Anonymous

Travels in Africa

Anonymous

Travels in Africa

ISBN/EAN: 9783337309176

Printed in Europe, USA, Canada, Australia, Japan

Cover: Foto ©Andreas Hilbeck / pixelio.de

More available books at **www.hansebooks.com**

TRAVELS IN AFRICA

REVISED BY THE EDITORS.

NEW YORK:
CARLTON & LANAHAN.
CINCINNATI: HITCHCOCK & WALDEN.
SUNDAY-SCHOOL DEPARTMENT.

PREFACE

TO

TRAVELS IN AFRICA.

———

Though the following is a very imperfect description of those parts of the African continent which are known, it may be relied on as a faithful abridgment of the accounts given by different travellers of veracity.

The object of uniting these separate accounts into one unbroken narrative must be obvious to every one. Though the person introduced, however, as the narrator, be a fictitious character, so far as it is connected with African travels, it is much to be apprehended that many such as he are to be found in every walk of life. Should one of them meet with this little book, and learn from it the lesson it is intended to give—that we should rest contented in that station in which almighty Wisdom has placed us—the Travels in Africa will not have been written in vain.

TRAVELS IN AFRICA.

There are few of the inhabitants of Dublin who have not, at one period or another, visited the country which lies south of that capital, and in which are situated the small village of Enniskerry and the watefall beyond it. Its beauty is so well known, that travellers have even gone from a distance to see it, and I believe no one could ever say he returned disappointed from his excursion. On the right, as you approach Enniskerry, lies a range of hills, which are called the Dublin Mountains. On the left is the fine expanse of sea which stretches between the Dunleary shore and the Hill of Howth : and in front you see the Killiney Hills, and the greater and less Sugar-loaf, so called from their resembling the shape in which white sugar is made up for sale. With such a sea and mountain prospect before you, it may be well supposed that man can do but little to increase its beauty, and yet, majestic as are these objects, they are, as it were, set off by the richly cultivated land which extends on all sides. Pleasure grounds, fields, and woods; the mansions of the wealthy, the populous village, the substantial farm-house, are scattered here and there at short distances from each other; and though along the roadside you will occasionally see cottages of a mean and neglected appearance, a stranger would say that the general appearance of the people betokened industry. I must acknowledge that we have too much reason to condemn the peasant who suffers a pool of water to collect before his door, when by a little care and attention the hollow might be filled up; who had sooner stop his broken window with dirty rags than have it mended with glass; and who lets the outside walls of his cabin remain quite black, when a few pennyworth of quicklime would make them look as neat as they are now filthy; but why should the slovenly habits of a few bring reproach on any but themselves? 'Tis true, you will now and then meet with a woman who seems as if she never used a comb or water, so blowzed is her hair under a very soiled cap, and so black her skin; but a man would not be telling truth, if he denied that by far the greater number are both neat and clean in their persons. 'Tis true, also, you might formerly have met troops of ragged dirty children shouting and playing along the road or in the villages, quarrelling with one another, and sometimes saying bad words—at present, however, the case is widely altered. Thanks be to those to whom God has given not alone the means, but the inclination to be useful, schools are set up in different places, where the young are taught to spend their time in another manner; they learn to read, to write, to cast accounts, to shun bad company, to do to others as they would wish to have done to themselves, and to read their Bibles. Their parents, also, however uninstructed they may be, know too well that ignorance is often the parent of vice, and that the surest way of calling down a blessing on their offspring is, to teach them honesty toward man, and piety toward God ; so that it is not too much to expect that a short time will see every one, however humble his condition, able to take up an instructive book after working hours, and to find a pleasure in reading it.

I said the country was sufficiently beautiful to attract even strangers from a distance, and though many a spot will engage attention, I think it would be difficult to point out one so highly interesting as the approach to the Scalp. This is a pass between two hills, which seem as if they had once been joined together, forming one mountain, and had been rent asunder by some violent earthquake ; thus showing us how God can, in one moment, perform what the art of man could never effect. These two hills now stand apart from each other, and a fair and spacious road runs between them, leading from Dublin to Enniskerry. This road is long and straight, and the traveller, in approaching the Scalp from Dublin, sees through it to the great Sugar-loaf Hill, which lies beyond, and seems to close the pass through which he would journey. From the Scalp to the foot of the Wicklow Hills stretches a beautiful fertile valley ; in which, at about two miles' distance, may be seen rising the smoke of the town of Enniskerry. In the fields, on the right you may still see the remains of what has once been a neat and comfortable farm-house, the scene of health and industry, and of domestic happiness, until children became disobedient, and two virtuous, honest, and industrious parents were left destitute, and worse than childless. They had spared no pains in bringing up their children, a boy and a girl, in habits of honesty and industry; but what is the profit of all a parent's care if children will not try to mend their own faults, and, by being good and dutiful, endeavour to repay their care and affection? It grieves me to say how wayward they both proved; but, perhaps, they may serve as a warning to others.

The girl left her father and mother, married against their will, and fell into poverty; and the boy quitted his home, and went to sea, enticed away by an old school-fellow and companion of his, who often, as they used to walk or work in the fields together, would tell him what a fine thing it would be to go abroad together and see foreign parts; and Tom sometimes lent an ear to him, and then they would lay out their plans together. But I must do Tom the justice to say, that often, after talking in this way, when he returned from work in the evening, and saw his home so cheerful, his father and mother sitting by the fire, awaiting him, and a cleanly comfortable supper ready to sit down to; and when he used to think how his sister Lucy had deserted them, his heart would smite him while he said to himself,—I never can resolve to quit such a happy home.

Many an hour of grief and sorrow Tom might have spared his poor parents and himself, if he had been steady enough to abide by these good feelings. If people considered how many blessings they have at home, and how thankful they should be for them, they would never, I am sure, quit their own country, and seek for happiness in foreign lands. So thought poor Tom when after ten years he returned once more to the foot of his Wicklow mountains, and found what alterations time had made during his absence. His poor mother had never held up her head after he quitted her, and a mound of earth in the neighbouring church-yard showed Tom her humble grave.

His father, thus left alone, at first gave way to his grief, and could not bear to stir himself about his farm, or look after his house; but Jackson was a good man, and had always read his Bible, and he knew what is required of us all, each in our own situation of life, and that there is no one, however humble, or poor, or unhappy, that has not his duties to perform: and that it would not be fulfilling his duty either to God or man to let his little farm go to ruin, and neglect all the blessings he still enjoyed. "Though the world should go hard with us, we have still religion to comfort us," said he, " and in God we have a friend who will never leave us." His health, indeed, declined, and he never was again the same hale, stout man he had been before his sorrows came on; but he was still to be seen engaged in his field, or working in his little garden. The place never again looked the same that it had done in his prosperous days; his good wife, who used to share all his labours, was dead—his children had both forsaken him, and after his day's toil on his farm he had but a lonely home to return to. The neighbours, however, were kind and friendly, and few ever passed by the farm house without calling to see him, and telling him the village news. Jackson himself seldom quitted his own little spot of ground to meddle in such matters, and yet he liked to hear what was going on in the world, and whenever any difficulty occurred, he had always a word of advice for an acquaintance. On a summer's evening he was always to be found, when labour was over, seated under an old thorn-tree which grew before the door, and which he himself had planted the day his son was born, thinking how his little child and this young plant might flourish alike. This was always his favourite seat in the summer evenings, and who will wonder that, at such a time, something like hope that Tom might yet return would now and then come across the old man's mind?

It was on such an evening as this that a neighbour, returning from the market at Bray, stopped as he was passing by Jackson's door, and told him he had heard of a person who had landed from a ship in the bay, and was making earnest inquiry after farmer Jackson, so that, says he, may be he might have news of Tom for you, and I'll send my boy to make inquiries, and, if you wish, to bring him to you. "No, neighbour, no," cries Jackson, "I'll go myself;" and starting up, he took the way across the fields to the next village, and in ten minutes afterward was clasped in his son's arms.

"Father, how will you ever forgive me for all the wrong I've done you? but I've paid dearly for it, in all I've suffered since I left you,"—these were Tom's first words; and again he begged his father's forgiveness; while poor Jackson could only think of the happiness of the present moment, and welcome his lost child home again.

They walked back together to the cottage, and there, for many an evening afterward, did Tom recite to his father all he had seen and gone through during the ten long years he had been away. "The day I left you, father," he began, "Jem Hobson and I made the best of our way to Dublin. He met an acquaintance as we were walking through the town, who told him he was going to sail for Liverpool that night, in the hopes he might be able to get work there. He was, like ourselves, dissatisfied with his lot, and thought any change must be for the better; but, as I was told afterward, he had good reason to say his own country was the best of all, for in a few months he returned without a penny in his pocket."

"I know he did," said farmer Jackson, "for

it was by his return I heard what had become of you."

"Well," said Tom, "Jem Hobson and I went down to the Pigeon House with him, about four o'clock in the evening, and we all three sailed that night. The weather was fine, the moonlight was bright, and I had a feeling such as I cannot describe to you; when I saw the fine ocean all around me, and felt that it could carry me all over the world, I thought myself the happiest fellow alive."

"Ay, Tom, so people always think, and so I once thought myself," said his father, "that to have *what we call our freedom* is the finest thing in the world; and so it is the first of blessings, when we enjoy *true freedom*, and when we know how to use it aright. But, Tom, tell me is that *true* freedom which a child obtains by casting off a parent's authority, disobeying and deserting him? You've cost me and your poor mother many a sorrowful hour; but it's all over now; her troubles are ended, and I trust, my son, so are mine. Young people always believe the world to be full of joy, until by experience they find it to be full of care."

"I believe you are right," said Tom, "for often I wondered afterward how I could ever have felt such pleasure in quitting my native land. We reached Liverpool in about thirty-six hours; Jem's friend got into work in a day or two, but it was not so easy a matter for Jem and me, who had not been trained up to any trade but the farming business, the harvest being all made up before we went there. We loitered about the town idle day after day, heartily tired of having nothing to do, and the little sum we had scraped together melting away by degrees: 'And is this,' thought I, 'what I have exchanged my father's comfortable cottage for, where, though potatoes and milk, and perhaps a bit of bacon on a Sunday was all we had to live upon, there was plenty of it, and kind neighbours about us: and here am I, poor and alone in this great town?' Still, I must own, we were not cured of our love of rambling. We might have returned home, but, like fools, we thought only of the laugh that would be raised against us; so, in order to escape that, we made bad worse, by resolving to go to sea. Once determined on this, there was no difficulty of putting it in practice. Liverpool is always crowded with merchant vessels, and as at that time there was a great want of hands, we soon engaged with a captain who was going on a distant voyage to South America; this, however, was no objection, for Jem and I cared not much where we went. At first he told us he had already as many men as his ship required, and that, at all events, he did not like engaging landsmen, on account of their ignorance of the sea-faring life; but being a humane man, and seeing that we were active and sober, and only wished to be industriously employed he at length consented to hire us. The ship was to sail the very next day. I remember the time, father, when I thought it would take a fortune to fit myself out for such a voyage as I was now about to commence, but times were changed with us, and Jem and I went on board the Caledonia with nothing but the clothes upon our backs. You will believe it, my heart almost failed me next day when I found myself leaving British ground, perhaps for ever; besides, you don't know what it is to trust one's self, almost for the first time, to the wide ocean, with nothing but a board between you and death.

"A fair wind from the north-east bore us down the channel, and for the first few days, except that I suffered dreadfully from sea-sickness, nothing occurred to make me repent of my voyage. It was on the 17th of June we sailed from Liverpool, and, as we had favourable breezes, our voyage went on prosperously for a while; to me every thing was new; and I wish I could remember now to tell you all the strange sights I saw; the very fish that swam by the ship, and the sea birds that flew over our heads, were all strange to me: and whichever way I turned, there was nothing around me but sky and water.

"We had been about a fortnight at sea when, in the evening, shortly before sunset, I heard the man at the mast-head cry out, 'Land.' I looked about me, but could see nothing like it, till at length one of the sailors pointed out what appeared to me only a faint cloud at a vast distance, which he told me was the Island of Madeira. By degrees, we approached nearer and nearer, and by the next morning came so close in that we could plainly see the different towns and villages along the coast; by and by we could distinguish, farther up the country, houses with the trees and gardens surrounding them, and I was told that when the wind blows off the land, the fine perfume of the orange trees with which the island abounds can be perceived out at sea to the distance of half a league. This was the first strange land I had ever seen: I longed of all things to go ashore, but the captain would not permit one of the men to leave the ship. Several boats came out to us from the island, the people civilly inviting us to land, and offering us a supply of water and provisions; but our ship was plentifully supplied with both. They offered us a kind of wine which is made there, and is very much liked by good judges, but we had no need of any.

"We anchored that night in the Bay of Funchal, which is the principal town in the island, and sailed again the next morning. The following day showed us a wonderfully high mountain, rising at a great distance from us, and called the Peak of Teneriffe. I can never forget the wonder with which I looked at it. I thought our Wicklow mountains very high, but they're only stepping stones compared to this one. We did not touch at the island, but bore down to the southward.

"For a few days we went on prosperously, and I became more and more satisfied with my condition; but I soon found that I was then experiencing only the sweets of a seaman's life, and that I knew nothing yet of its hardships; though hard enough I used to think it, at first, to be obliged to climb up the shrouds, until my head grew giddy; and I, who never knew what it was to be without my warm comfortable bed to sleep the whole night in, was now forced to be content to lie for a couple of hours at a time, when it came to my turn, and to work hard, day and night, wet or dry, hot or cold. But this, I found, was nothing to what sailors have sometimes to endure. Shortly after this, it was on the second of July, about noon, there was every appearance of a violent storm coming on. The sky grew dark, the wind rose, and the waves began to swell. The captain called out to every man to do his duty. Never shall I forget the scene that followed. The storm became in a few hours so violent, and the ship tossed so, that I thought she would have gone down between every sea. The whole of the next night we continued in this dreadful situation, the waves dashing over us every moment, and the wind blowing with such fury, that we began to be apprehensive lest we should be driven on the shore of Africa. We fired several guns, as signals of distress, but there was not a vessel in sight; and if you could have witnessed the scene that was before us when daylight dawned, nothing around us but waves rolling mountain high, and the men, who but two days before looked so stout-hearted and hardy, now worn out with fatigue, you would have pitied us. The captain was the only man who looked like himself, but he was steady to the last. For my part, overcome with terror, I could only implore the Almighty to preserve us. I promised that if it would please him to restore me to my home again, I never would quit it more. I thought of you and my poor mother; I thought of all the good you had ever taught me, and believed a judgment was come upon me for having deserted you; but it was now too late for such reflections. In the morning early some of the seamen had thought they could discern land at a great distance, and a few hours proved them to be right. At noon I had occasion to go below, when a cry of 'land,' was raised; again I hastened upon deck, and could plainly distinguish a long line of coast to the south-east; but we had no means of either guiding the ship, or judging whereabouts we were. Rudder, anchor, and compass were gone. However, the sight of land cheered us a little.

"But it was just at this moment, when hope had somewhat returned to us, that we found ourselves surrounded by dangers we had little expected. Upon sounding, the captain began to fear by the shallowness of the water, that we were near sand banks. Shortly after we touched upon one, and though, by lowering the sails, lightening the vessel, and taking down the topgallant mast and top-mast, we soon succeeded in setting the ship afloat again, we were in continual fear every moment lest we should come upon another. In about an hour afterward we did so, with such a shock as I thought would have knocked the ship to pieces. All our efforts to set her free again were now quite in vain: every thing was done to lighten her, the few guns she carried were thrown overboard; we cut down the mast; we tried half the day to set her afloat again, and sometimes you'd think she was quite free: she swung so loosely, her stern alone touched a little; but, from the violence of the winds and waves, it was impossible to disengage her entirely. At length one of the men from below was heard to cry out that she had sprung a leak. All hands hastened to the pumps, but to no purpose; the water came in faster than we could work it out, and in less than an hour she filled nearly as high as the lower deck hatchway.

"The captain now, seeing that all was over, declared he would not leave the ship to the last, but ordered the boats to be hoisted over, and we threw into them such provisions as we could find, in the hurry and confusion of the moment; some casks of biscuit and flour, and a small supply of water. A few of the men jumped into them, and had orders from the captain to keep them under the lee of the ship, and to be ready to receive the crew when every effort should fail: the whole of the crew consisted of about nine and the captain.

"The storm now raged with increased violence, the ship filled worse and worse, and threatened every instant to go to pieces. At length, the captain called out to every man to save himself. O, father, such a scene as there was then; almost every one flew to the boats except poor Jem Hobson:—in the hurry and terror of the moment, his first idea was to save himself by swimming; he sprang into the sea before our eyes, and not even at the same side of the ship that the boats were lying at, for then we might, perhaps, have saved him, though the waves ran tremendously high. I saw him rise twice; I threw him an oar—he could not reach it—I threw him a rope; he caught at it, but the other end had not been made fast to the ship; it gave way with him, and I never saw him more. I was in the act of springing into the sea after him, when some person grasped my arm, and forcibly dragged me, crying out, 'What keeps you here, every one's gone but you?' And sure enough, when I turned around, I saw that there was not a creature on board with me but one. 'We both now leaped into one of the boats, together, and, in a few minutes, the ship went to pieces before our eyes. It is a sorrowful sight to see a fine noble-looking ship, built so strong that you might think it would last for ever, and which, as they told me, had gone twice around the world, before ever I saw her—to see her knocked about by the waves, until there were hardly two planks of her together."

"How wonderful are the ways of Providence, my son; thus it is that the mightiest works of man come to an end; and yet who need wonder they should, when God ordained that even this earth, and every thing else that he created, shall one time or other be destroyed. But, Tom, tell me how far were you from that shore that you had seen: and were you able to reach it before night?"

"We rowed hard all the day long, for we dreaded night coming upon us in our open boats, and in such a dreadful sea. Sometimes we were so nearly under water, that you would think we were going to the bottom: then the waves would carry up the boat almost as high as the clouds. In this way we toiled for hour after hour. We had plenty of oars, for the captain had been careful to throw into the boats every thing he could lay his hands on, that he thought we might want. Why, father, one active man like him does more good at such a time than twenty others. There was Jem Hobson, who, all the time the ship was in danger, never did a hand's turn to save her, and then, after all, to jump into the sea just like a madman!

"It was growing dusk when we reached the shore, which was a very rocky one. There was no easy landing, such as I had at Liverpool; but from the force of the sea, the boats were lifted up by a prodigious wave, and laid high and dry upon the beach: and seeing no kind of habitation at all near, we lashed them fast to the rocks, with what cordage we had with us, in order that we might have the means of escaping if any thing should happen to us; though if we had been obliged to venture out to sea in the open boats, we saw nothing before us but the chance of their being swamped. We laid ourselves down to sleep upon the shore, one of us at a time keeping watch through the night, for fear of any wild beasts coming upon us, and we kept close beside us what fire-arms we had."

" But, Tom, I hope the first thing you all did was to thank God for having so mercifully saved you." " Indeed, father, our hearts were filled with gratitude, and I trust the prayers we then offered up to him proceeded from men duly affected by his undeserved mercy.

" We rested but badly, as you may suppose; the fatigue of working the ship had been so great that any one might think we could have slept upon a rock; but some of us had thrown off both jackets and shoes, that we might, if necessary, the more easily swim ashore; we were covered with bruises, the waves had so knocked us about: completely drenched with the sea water, and without shelter, and besides all this, the place on which we were cast had the appearance of a desert; not a tree was in sight; no grass, not even a hill, nor, in short, any thing but sand, as far as the eye could reach; and to add to all our sorrows, the captain told us we were on the coast of Africa. We afterward found it was a few miles south of Cape Blanco, which is on the western coast of Africa, and in the twentieth degree of latitude."

" Well, but, Thomas, the blacks were kind to you, I hope; a shipwrecked man well deserves pity, and none but a savage would refuse it."

"That's true," said the son, "but that's exactly what the people are, who live in this part of Africa. They go almost naked, wearing only a rug or skin around their waist, their upper parts, and from the knees downward, being quite bare of covering; their hair is not curled and woolly, like the blacks whom you sometimes see, but very long and straight; those that we saw were called Moors, and live in tents made of woven goats' hair. They frequently remove from one place to another, according to the season of the year, or the convenience of pasturage. In the month of February, when the heat of the sun scorches up every sort of vegetation, they strike their tents, and approach the Negro country, to the south, where they reside till the rain commences in the month of July. At this time, having purchased corn and other necessaries in exchange for salt, they again depart northward, and continue in the desert till the rains are over."

"This wandering and restless way of life," said Jackson, "must inure their bodies to hardships."

"Yes, it does," said Tom, "but it renders them fierce and unsocial. Cut off from all intercourse with their more industrious neighbours, whom they are more ready to plunder than to trade with, they never show kindness to any but those of their own tribe or nation, and seem to consider all the rest of mankind as their natural enemies. Such are the vices of human nature, when unacquainted with true religion. During the time they remain south of the desert, they hover about the coast for the purpose of plundering any vessels which suffer shipwreck, and of seizing such of the crew as survive, in order to make them slaves.

"But, father, why should you wonder that these ignorant heathens show no mercy to the poor shipwrecked seamen, when, in our own country, we sometimes hear of the same barbarity. I met a man in the ship that brought me to England, who said he had been once cast away on the western coast of Ireland, and that the people came down to the wreck in great crowds, and not only stripped him, but actually took every thing they could lay their hands on. I could not believe it: I told him it was false; for I felt myself roused at such a charge against my countrymen. I said no Christian could be found so barbarous."

"Ay, Thomas," said old Jackson, "I wish that every one who calls himself a Christian, would act as such; but how many do not! I have often heard myself of such doings, and don't know how men who are unmerciful to their fellow creatures can hope to receive mercy from God. But I suppose the man you had accused of falsehood struck you?"

"No, indeed," said Thomas, "he did not; and it was not for want of courage either, for he had been in many a sea fight; but he was a sensible man, and very religious. I never shall forget the mild check he gave me : 'Another man, Thomas,' said he, 'would perhaps give you a sound threshing for calling him a liar; but I think that a very foolish, and I know it is a very wrong way of settling a dispute; besides, it wouldn't convince you, after all, that I was right. But look at this,' added he, (showing me the mark of a great cut which he had in his arm,) 'I got this because I resisted three of them who endeavoured to strip me.' But to return to my story. As soon as it is known through the country that a ship has been wrecked, and that any part of the cargo has been saved by the inhabitants of the coast where the catastrophe happened, a market is immediately opened, to which the Arabs who live in the northern parts of Africa come from a great distance to buy the plunder; but they are much more knowing than those who sell, who are so extremely ignorant that they will dispose of the most valuable articles for a mere trifle. I saw English bank notes exchanged for a few dates, a fruit that grows in great plenty in Barbary and Morocco; the buyer cunningly pretending that they were nothing but pieces of waste paper. Watches, clothes, muslins, silks, linens, they gladly barter for horses, camels, or any of the very few articles which their wretched way of living requires. They, however, know the value of guns and pistols, swords, bits of old iron and nails, and don't part with them so readily. However, you must not think every thing goes on smoothly with these robbers; they often find the truth of the old proverb—that honesty is the best policy. It sometimes happens, when the crew and cargo of a wreck fall into the hands of a party who are too weak to defend their prize, that a stronger party attacks them, and, after much bloodshed, either carries off every thing by force, or obliges them to surrender their plunder for what is far below the value they put on it. However, the next morning, at daybreak, we were surrounded by about fifty of these savages, and made prisoners. From the wreck they got little more than the iron works; for the vessel having bilged, the cargo was almost entirely lost. Here we stayed thirteen days; in fact, as long as the Moors thought it likely that any more of the wreck would be washed ashore. We also suffered much from hunger, fish being the only food we had; so that, when the weather was bad, we were in danger of starving. The mode of dressing the fish is by cutting it into pieces, and letting it broil on the hot sand by the sun's heat. Among the things that floated ashore was a chest which contained some fishing lines and hooks; but though we offered to teach them their use, they refused to be instructed.

"Immediately after we had been made prisoners, they stripped us; hiding our clothes in the sand, for fear that some stronger tribe would come and seize them. Being thus exposed to the sun, our bodies became dreadfully blistered. In Ireland you can have no idea of the heat we endured; indeed, it is more like the glow which is felt on putting your hand inside an oven. At night we had no dew; but the air still continued so hot that we were obliged to dig holes in the sand to sleep in, for the sake of coolness. Add to this, we were soon covered with vermin; for the Moors actually swarmed with them.

"About a week after the shipwreck, our captain died; a better seaman never stepped a deck, and until we left the ship, and saw her going to pieces, he bore up like a man, and set us all an example of courage and resignation; but from the moment he set foot on shore he began to droop. He had been all his life at sea, and, by great industry, had saved some money; for being always a sober, careful man, the merchants were ever anxious to employ him. He had ventured his all in the vessel; and when he saw the fruit of so much labour swallowed up by the waves, he could not, he said, survive it. One of my shipmates told me he had left a wife and two children in Liverpool, and that he had the name of a good husband, father, and friend."

"Thomas," said his father, "the captain ought to have borne misfortune better; in this world it is often our lot to suffer; and happy is the man whose sorrows are not caused by his own misconduct: but we should always be resigned, and say, 'The will of God be done.' Had he, in place of giving way to useless sorrow, exerted himself, and hoped for the best, he might have been, like you, telling all he saw and suffered to his family. But did the Moors treat him ill?"

"Yes, they did. They knew he was our captain, and foolishly thought he had hid a great many articles in the sand. They used sometimes to beat him, and leave him exposed to the weather at night, by way of forcing him to give up all; so that at last, partly from bad treatment, and partly from not exerting himself, he died. A few days after, we who survived him were near falling under the hands of the savages who had seized us. In sharing the spoil, they fell out among themselves, and immediately began to fight most ferociously. What an alteration does anger make in the human face! They gnashed their teeth at each other, they gave the most hideous yells; their eyes were red and fiery, and, in short, they looked like any thing rather than human beings. Nor must you suppose our situation to have been free from danger during the dispute: they dragged us from side to side; they cut at each other over our heads, making their crooked swords, which are called scimitars, whiz through the air, almost within an inch of us; the blood, streaming from every gash, ran down their naked bodies, increasing the frightfulness of their appearance. I was too much in fear of my life to think much; but when I afterward brought it to mind, I thought what a dreadful passion anger must be, when it can be the cause of so much cruelty, and I firmly resolved to strive against it. A division of the prisoners being made among the conquerors, the mate, another man, named Williams, and I were left in possession of twenty Moors, who immediately prepared to leave the coast. They had four camels, three of which carried water, and the other fish, which was to be our food, and the baggage. We sometimes travelled fifteen miles a day; and this continued for about thirty days, during which time we did not meet a human being, and saw nothing but sand. We then reached a spot, lying, as I believe, nearly due east of the place which we had left, where we found about thirty tents."

"But why," said Jackson, "would you load the camels with water? Surely, in so long a journey you must have met with many a spring of water."

"Not a drop," answered Thomas : " the part of Africa through which we passed was a great desert. I heard it was compared to an ocean of sand, through which you might travel for months together, without seeing a spot fit for a man to live in, or finding a drop of water. The people, therefore, who are obliged to cross this wide waste must carry with them as much as will serve them until they reach the very few wells which are scattered over the country, at great distances from each other. Nor must you wonder at the scarcity of water in a place where the sun is so hot as to burn up the few things which grow in so sandy a soil; indeed, the ground becomes so burning that the negroes themselves can scarcely bear, during the midday heat, to stand on it with their naked feet."

"However," said Jackson, "it must be unwise to use such large beasts as camels. I should think they could scarcely carry water enough for their own drinking, much less for those who are travelling with them."

"Father," said Thomas, "the more we see, the more we ought to bless God for all his mercies. Unless he had given them the camel, this desert would have been entirely impassable ; but with it they can take the longest journeys, the animal not needing water for twelve or fifteen days at a time : indeed, it has been called the ship of the desert. Before it sets out, it drinks a great quantity, which remains, as if in a store cask, quite sweet and good, until the creature wants it to moisten its food. His master knows this, and will sometimes kill a camel, if hard pressed, in order to get the water that is in the stomach ; a thing that is likely to occur very often, when we think how many accidents may happen to delay their coming to each of the wells at the time expected, particularly when they have no path to guide them. Its feet are very broad, partly divided, and the sole consists of a tough elastic cushion : a structure which keeps the creature from sinking in the sand. There are seven hard thick lumps, one upon the breast, two on each fore leg, and one upon each hind leg. On these the camel rests when kneeling to sleep, or to receive its burden. I learned also the many things which the camel is useful for ; the Moors made very fine stuffs from the hair ; the skin gave them good leather ; they ate the flesh, and drank the milk, which are both very wholesome; and even the dung gave them firing, when dried. Its food, also, is very easily produced. Grass or corn it never wants, nor, indeed, are they to be had in such a country; it eats the coarsest weeds and shrubs, and prefers the nettle and the thistle to the finest pasture.

"Is not the hand of Providence in this, Thomas?" said his father. "It loves that food which is to be had in abundance, and cares nothing for that which grows too sparingly to satisfy its appetite!"

"When the Moors," continued Thomas, "are about to set out on a journey through the desert, they fill with water a number of goat-skins, which, after being taken whole from the carcass of the animal, they sew up, leaving the neck only open. These they sling, by the skin of their legs, on each side of the camel; they next, by a girth, which passes under the camel's belly, fasten on their baskets for the women and children to ride in; these are made of camels' skins, and fixed in such a manner upon a frame, with a wooden rim around the top, that three or four can sit in them with great safety, only taking care to keep their balance. The men ride on saddles, which are placed on the camel's back, just before the hump, and fastened on by a girth.

For a week after our arrival, my companion and I were allowed to rest; at the end of this time, we were set to keep sheep and goats. The mate, however, soon after left us, being obliged to accompany his master, who went on a journey northward, nor did we long remain behind. The Moors often set out on what they call slaving expeditions : that is, after going some distance from home, they hide in the neighbourhood of some negro town, and carry off any of the inhabitants they can lay their hands on; and it was upon one of these enterprises we set out. We were thirty Moors, Williams and myself, and we brought with us twelve camels loaded with water, barley, and flour. In ten days we thought we should reach a place where there was water, but the season was uncommonly hot, so that when we arrived we found the well quite dry. We were therefore forced to put ourselves upon short allowance for the remaining four days of our journey, which brought us to Soudenny. Here we hid ourselves for several days, and at length seized a woman and three children, whom we found walking in the evening near the town."

" But what kind of a place is it, Tom, where the people go out in that way to kidnap each other ?"

" I don't wonder at the question, father ; but since it is so, does it not show us how happy *we* are who live in a Christian country, where no man, however rich or grand, can hurt even his poorest neighbour ? We did not, however, long remain concealed. One evening our party was surrounded by fifty Negroes, armed with daggers, and bows and arrows. Our Moors were a cowardly set, for, though well armed, they scarcely made any resistance. After firing a single shot, by which a boy was wounded, we were all made prisoners, and carried into the town. Here we remained some days previous to being sent to Tombuctoo, where the king resided. The Moors were confined in a spot surrounded by a mud wall, only six feet high, and could have made their escape easily, but they appeared to me never to think of it.

" The village of Soudenny contains about fifty houses, built of clay, the roofs being also of clay, laid on sticks. How comfortless these savages live, thought I, when I saw them; they have no chairs or tables in them, nor any vessels except wooden bowls. The better class wear a kind of frock of blue nankeen, but neither shoes, hats, nor turbans; the chief has a gold ornament worked on the shoulders of his frock; some had gold ear-rings in their ears, and also large oval rings, which passed through a hole bored in the gristly part of the nose, and hung down to the mouth. They use bows and arrows, and are very expert in hitting a small mark at the distance of about twenty yards.

" While we remained here, I had an opportunity of seeing a Negro funeral; it was that of the young lad who had been wounded by the shot fired by our party. Four men carried the body on their shoulders, and laid it in a neighbouring tent; it was a pitiful sight to see his poor mother walking on before, quite frantic with grief, clapping her hands and crying out as she went along, ' Good child! good child! he never told a lie, no, never, never!' and all the people that stood by showed their grief by screaming and howling. I thought what a lesson this was to us, when even these poor ignorant people have such a regard for truth, and how much less excusable our sin must be in telling a lie, living as we do in a country where we are taught how wicked it is, and have plenty of good examples before us, if we would but follow them; but we are all more ready to take after the bad than the good; and moreover, I often think, father, that we are a great deal more apt to talk of other people's faults than to set about mending our own."

"All that's true, Tom; but think, likewise, what encouragement it is to children to speak truth when they see how the recollection of their never having told a lie is such a comfort to their parents when they lose them. Think of this poor woman, even in all her sorrow, finding relief in the thought that while her child lived he had never told a lie. I am sure, if any of her other children were standing by when she said it, it must have made them resolve that, for the future, nothing should ever tempt them to tell any thing contrary to truth. Did you see the boy's funeral, or do you know whether they bury their dead as we do?"

"The young man that I speak of lay in the tent all day, and in the dusk of the evening they carried him out, dug a grave and laid him in it; they then planted over it a particular kind of shrub, from which no stranger is afterward allowed to pull a leaf or even to touch it.

"In about fifteen days we arrived at our destination: many of the Moors having been beheaded during the journey for attempting to escape. Here we were presented to the king and queen, who sent the surviving Moors to prison, but kept my companion and myself in their own house, where we were treated with the greatest kindness. It was quite plain that they had never seen white men before, for they used often to sit looking at us for hours together. The people also flocked in crowds to stare at us, and I afterward heard that many came several days' journey for that purpose."

"Ay, Thomas, that is just what we do ourselves, when a stranger comes among us; we think ourselves far more sensible than the blacks, and yet I recollect once, in Dublin, there was a black woman showed—I think they called her a Hottentot—and so curious were the people about her that they used to pay money to see her."

"I believe, father, you will find that we do many things besides that, which are little better than what the Africans do. But to continue; near the town of Tombuctoo, which I should tell you is the capital of the country, there flows a large river, on which I saw canoes, made of fig trees hollowed out, and able to carry about three men. The corn grows about six feet high, with a bushy head, as large as a pint bottle; the grain, however, being small; this they grind between two stones, and having sifted, boil it into a thick stirabout; the natives then

Africa.   p. 37.

Hottentot Woman.

sit upon the ground, men, women, and children, around this mess, to which goats' milk has been added, and eat it with their fingers; even the king and queen do the same, having neither spoons, knives, nor forks.

" These people have no horses, but they have instead a kind of camel which, though unfit for carrying loads, is very fleet, and will carry a man for days together, at the rate of fifty miles a day. It is this animal they use in hunting the elephant, which you know is the largest four-footed animal in the world. I recollect one evening, I was endeavouring, by the help of a few words which I picked up, to talk to a Negro, when we heard a whistling noise at a distance: the Negro immediately gave me to understand it was an elephant, and the next morning we followed his tracks in pursuit of him, mounted on our two camels, and armed only with bows and arrows; the latter were pointed with iron, very sharp, and dipped in a black liquor prepared from some herb, which is a deadly poison. I followed till my comrade got within three quarters of a mile of his game; but his prodigious size frightened me, for it was the first I had ever seen; he was at least twelve feet high, and his legs were as thick as my body. The Negro, however, far from being frightened, set his camel at full speed, and riding past, shot an arrow, which struck the animal in the head. The elephant instantly started forward to pursue his hunter, dashing his trunk against the ground with violence, and making a dreadful roaring, which might have been heard at a great distance. The camel, thus followed, ran the faster from fear, so that the elephant was soon left behind, and about three days after, he was found lying on the ground in a dying state, and not very far from the place where he had been shot. The Negroes eat the flesh, which they cut from the legs and the hinder parts of the body, with great relish; but I never could like it; it was very coarse grained, and had a strong flavour.

"The people of Tombuctoo are both stout and healthy, for they will lie out in the sun in midday, and also sleep without shelter at night, though a heavy fog, which comes from the river, falls like dew upon the ground. They also grease their bodies with butter, which makes the skin smooth and shining, but if they neglect it, it will grow rough and very ugly.

"The men all have the marks of a deep cut on the forehead reaching down to the nose, from which others branch out at each side over the eyebrows, into which, while the wound is fresh, they put a blue die, which never afterward washes out; but they are very dirty in their habits, for sometimes they will not wash themselves for fourteen days together. The king and queen changed their dress once a week."

"But I hope, Thomas," said Jackson, "you never fell into their custom; cleanliness, I have often remarked, shows a cheerful disposition, and, says an old proverb, is next to godliness;

however, that, you may say, is going too far; but this much I know, that would we consult health or comfort, we would strive, as much as possible, to be clean in our cabins and in our persons. Water surely is cheap enough, for it costs nothing, and it would appear as if Providence made it plentiful to encourage our using it freely."

"That is quite my opinion too," said Tom; "I remember being once told that if a man meets with an accident, and has no way of getting to the doctor, let him only keep the wound clean, and cover it up from the air, and it will get well in half the time it otherwise would; so I never failed, night and morning, to wash in the river.

"The marriages are very curious; the only form being, that the girl goes to the king's house, and stays there until after sunset, when the man who is to be her husband goes to fetch her away. This is followed by a wedding feast and a dance. A man, however, is not confined to one wife, he may have several, and the consequence you may well guess—there is no peace at home, the women are always quarrelling and fighting, and the husband instead of the affection which he ought to feel, and would feel, if he had but one wife, as with us, loves none of them. When parents become very old and unable to work, their children must support them; but if they are childless, there is a house in which they live, four or five in a room, at the king's expense."

"Have they any public diversions, Tom?" asked Jackson.

"Yes: their favourite one is dancing, and this they will often begin two hours before sunset, and continue all night; this takes place once a week, when a hundred or more come together. They dance in a circle, usually around a fire, and their music is a fife and tambourine, but every one engaged sings also, as loud as he can, so that the noise is almost deafening.

"But to go on with my story;—during the six months that we stayed at Tombuctoo, I and my comrade never met with any thing but civility and kindness, for they looked on us as friends. We had as much food as we wanted, and no work; but the Moors who were taken with us were kept in prison the whole time. There now, however, came a party of their countrymen to ransom them and us, and the price they paid was five camels' load of tobacco. Accordingly, two days after, we set out and kept along the side of the river for ten days, striking farther toward the middle parts of Africa."

"But were you able to tell the course you went?"

"Yes: you know the sun always rises in the east and sets in the west; so, at least, twice a day you know the points of the compass; but also, when the sun is at its height, if you turn your back to it, your face will be opposite to the north; and I always gave great heed to this, for I never gave up the hope of making my escape from the savages. At the end of this time we left the river, having first loaded our camels with water, and went north for a fortnight, travelling about eighteen miles a day. This brought us to Tandeny, where we fortunately found great treasures—not gold, or silver, or diamonds, but what is far more precious in a country like this, four wells of excellent water, and some large ponds of salt water. There we stopped a fortnight, to rest the ransomed Moors, who, from long confinement, had become very weak; we also sold one of our camels for two sacks of dates and an ass, and having loaded the four remaining camels with water, we again set out to cross the desert in a north-east direction. But how shall I tell you all our sufferings? for nine and twenty days we travelled on without meeting a single human being; the whole way being a sandy flat, without tree, shrub, or grass. After going on for about fourteen days, at the rate of eighteen miles daily, we began to grow weak; our stock of water ran short, and our provisions were nearly exhausted; our ass died of fatigue, but this was a seasonable relief, for we cut it up, and laid it on one of the camels, where it dried in the sun, and served us for food."

" And did you like ass's flesh?"

" Why, you know a hungry man will not be very nice in his choice; but I recollect I thought it as good as goose."

" Well, but you shortly reached a watering place?"

"We did, sir," answered Thomas, "at the end of six days: but think of our distress when we found the well quite dry, owing to the heat of the season. At this time we had but eight gallons of water remaining; we were at least ten days' distance from a supply; and upon the small quantity we had, twenty-seven persons, the number of which our party consisted, had to live. We were therefore obliged to do what is usual in cases of necessity, we mixed our eight gallons with camel's urine, and thus were enabled to have a pint of liquor a day ourselves, and to give a quart daily to each of the camels. This, however, was not sufficient for the unfortunate Moors, who had been in confinement; in a short time, three of them lay down, unable to proceed; we then placed them on the camels, but they could not bear the uneasy motion, so they again attempted to walk, but could not. In the morning they were found dead in the place where they had lain down at night, and we left them there, without burial.

"How many gloomy thoughts came across my mind, as we sat out from the spot where they were lying. Our party, you would say, was a large one, but we were in the midst of a great, and to me it seemed an endless desert, as far as our sight extended, and there was nothing to prevent the view, nothing but sand and sky, and it made me think we were but a little speck in the creation. We said but little to each other, we felt as if we were alone; and if I had not put my trust in Him who is merciful, I should have given myself up to despair. The next day another Moor lay down, and, like his companions, perished. On the following day a Moor remained behind, in hopes that he who had dropped the day before might still come up and be able to join the party. At this time it was believed, what was found to be the fact, we were within a day's march of the town to which we were proceeding; but neither of the Moors ever afterward made his appearance, and I have no doubt they perished.

" The first fortnight we were allowed to rest from our fatigues ; but as soon as we had gained a little strength, we were, as before, set to take care of goats and sheep. We could now talk a little Moorish, and we frequently begged our masters to bring us to Serena, where we hoped to be ransomed by Europeans ; this they promised to do if we were attentive, but, at the end of eleven months, having waited patiently all that time, we found there was no appearance of it, so we spoke to them again, and were then given to understand, that, as they had been disappointed of getting slaves, in some of their late expeditions, they were determined to keep us. All this time we were suffering severely, exposed during the day to a scorching sun, almost in a state of nakedness : our food, however, though very plain, was in abundance, for we had plenty of barley flour and goats' milk. I now seriously entertained the design of attempting my escape ; and, accordingly, the next time I was sent with a camel to the well to draw water, instead of returning, I pushed on to reach a place called Wednoon, which I had been told was the name of the next town, and lay toward the north, in the direction of Mogadore, a town on the north-west coast of Africa, where I had heard there were English merchants living. I travelled the whole of that day, and would have continued to go on during the night, but the camel had been used to rest at night, and he refused to proceed. I used blows and entreaties, but all to no purpose; he lay down in the sand, and I was obliged to submit, expecting every moment to see my master's approach, who of course would use me with tenfold cruelty for attempting to escape; besides, I was alone in the midst of a desert, I had no track to guide me, and even though I should proceed, I could not tell whether the course I had taken would lead me to a town or not. Fatigued, hungry, and almost despairing, I tied the camel's fore foot close to his body, with the rope which fastened on the saddle, (the usual way of preventing these animals from straying far,) and lay down beside him. But never shall I forget the check I received for my mistrust in Providence. Looking upon the ground, I saw a small plant growing in such beauty, as to engage my attention for some time, during which I almost forgot my own situation. Does not the Almighty, thought I, who planted, watered, and has made to grow in this remote part of the world, a thing of such small value, look with compassion upon the sufferings of his own creatures? and may I not hope, if it is his will, to pass unhurt through even greater dangers than any that have yet happened to me? Perhaps such a thought will seem to you more than might be expected from one who had, till the time he left home, thought but little of God. I had been giddy, but all I had gone through, and the belief that I could never escape from slavery, unless by steadiness and exertion, had made me thoughtful: however, it was the sight of that little plant that revived me when almost in despair.

"The next morning, at daybreak, I started up, mounted the camel once more, and at nine o'clock saw at a little distance the smoke of a village; and, soon after, about a hundred Moors, who, with their faces turned to the east, as is their custom, were engaged in prayer. I thought myself safe, and had just inquired the way to the governor's house, when, looking behind me, I saw two camels coming up, and on one of them my master, who with a friend had set out in chase of me, and now claimed me as his slave. I now resolved that, come what would, I would never go back with him. We were accordingly brought before the chief, whose name was Mohammed, and who, having heard from me that my master had broken his promise of taking me to Mogadore, where I knew I should be released—which, indeed, to do him justice, he did not deny—decided in my favour, and told my master that he must resign me to him, at the price of a camel and a bushel of dates. My master loudly complained, but when he was told that if he refused he should get nothing, he at last consented, and made me over to him.

"The people of this place, which is called El Kabla, and lies still nearer the sea, advancing from Tombuctoo in a north-west direction, were better clothed and not so savage as those I had left. I was now set to tend camels, but in a fortnight after I was employed in taking care of goats. My work was light, and as I got nothing but kind treatment, my time passed pleasantly enough. At the end of six months, my master agreed to part with me, for about ten pounds' worth of blankets and dates, and I now became the property of a trader, who belonged to a village nearer the sea. It was a great way off, and the desert, I supposed, was again to be crossed before we could reach it; but I thought little of that, since it would bring me many days' journey nearer to the place where I might hope to be set free, or, at the worst, attempt to make my escape. The day after the bargain was made, I set out with a party of six men and four camels for a place called Woled, a village lying to the north-west, where we arrived after travelling for nine days, at the rate of about eighteen miles daily. On the road we met neither houses nor human beings; but the ground, contrary to my expectation, was covered with grass and shrubs. At Woled we found about fifty tents; and it was then that I was encouraged in the hope of being released from slavery. Shortly after our arrival, a Moor told my master that it was usual for the British consul at Mogadore to send to Wednoon, where this Moor lived, to purchase the Christians who were prisoners in the country; he therefore offered my master, as he was about to go there himself, to take me with him, in order to sell me for his account. This was agreed to, and in a few days I was advancing nearer and nearer, as I thought, to liberty.

"We went at a brisk rate, for we had each a camel, and in nine days came to Mouessa. This was by far the largest place I had seen, where there were no houses, for there were not less than one hundred tents; and here I was, as usual, set to tend camels; time was heavy on my hands, and I saw no preparations for our going to Wednoon. I heard there were other Christians there; and as it was the place where I might hope to get free, it will not surprise you, that after I had made inquiry into the course I was to follow, and the distance, I one evening set out on foot and alone, determined to desert. I had a very small quantity of goat's flesh with me, but I relied on getting a supply at some of the villages which I had heard were on the road. I had been very careful not to raise a suspicion of my design; and whenever I made any inquiries concerning Wednoon, had endeavoured to do it without observation.— But in this I was disappointed. When my master missed me, he found several who now called to mind that I had often asked questions respecting Wednoon, and he accordingly sent three men, mounted, to pursue me. I had travelled all night, and until about noon the next day, when they overtook me. I expected to be severely handled for my attempt, but they contented themselves with bringing me back to Mouessa; from whence, in a very short time after, Abdallah, my master's friend, and I set out, well mounted, and after travelling for five days, reached Wednoon, the place I had so long desired to see. How providential was it that I had been overtaken! for the whole time that we were on the road, we did not find a single house; so that had I gone on, as it was my design, I must have perished with hunger.

"Wednoon is a small town, consisting of about forty houses and some tents. The former are built chiefly of clay and stone, and several have a story above the ground floor. The ground was better tilled also than any I had seen in Africa, and produced plenty of corn and tobacco, there were also date and fig trees, grapes, apples, pears, and pomegranates. But think how great was my satisfaction to meet in the Christians whom I found there my old shipmates, who had been wrecked with me near Cape Blanco! They told me that they had been for some months in Wednoon, and were the property of the governor's son.

"Soon after our arrival, Abdallah offered me for sale to the chief, but the price could not be agreed on; so I was sold to Bel Cossion for seventy dollars' worth of blankets, gunpowder.

and dates. The only other white man at Wednoon was a Frenchman, who told me he had been wrecked on the neighbouring coast twelve years before; he had turned Mohammedan, and now lived in the country, with a wife and child and slaves, and gained a good living by making and selling gunpowder."

" Do you mean by that, Tom, that he had denied his religion?"

" Yes, father; the Moors are great bigots, and think that we are infidels, because we don't believe the same that they do. We also think them pagans; and how pleasing it is to *know* that *we* are in the right. When a Christian is made prisoner by them and sold as a slave, they generally do all they can by cruelty and bad treatment of every kind to make him turn, in order, by this means, to escape persecution; and as the consequence of becoming a Mohammedan is, that the person becomes immediately free, it too often happens that some among their captives do not resist the temptation; but when once they change their religion they can never leave the country; they must make up their minds to live and die there, for if caught making their escape, they would be put to death. Indeed, when I was in Barbary, some months after this, I heard of the master of a vessel, who, for some cause, having been condemned to death by the bashaw of Tripoli, thought to save his life by renouncing his religion. Instead, however, of being set free, as he expected, the governor only wished him joy that he was now one of what he called the true faith, and gave orders that he should be immediately executed. The Frenchman whom I speak of had gone very early to sea ; his parents, he told me himself, had never taken any pains to teach him his duty to God, and you see what was the consequence."

" Ay, Tom, if we would hold fast by religion, God would not desert us in this world, and we should be eternally happy in the next."

" The work in which I was here employed was building walls, making up fences, and working in the corn fields and in the tobacco plantations, of which there are a great many near the town. On the Moors' Sabbath we were not asked to work, and it was then my companions in slavery and I used to talk together: they had met with many adventures since we had parted, having been carried different ways ; and in telling them to each other we passed away many an hour."

" Do you recollect any of what they told you, Tom? I think their stories must have been worth hearing."

" With one exception, they were pretty nearly the same as my own. They had passed as slaves from one hand to another ; they had travelled over different parts of the dreary desert ; they had often been near perishing for want of water when they failed to light upon the particular spot where the wells are situated, a mistake not at all unlikely to happen when you consider that they had no path or road to follow; for, just like a ship at sea, their going over it leaves no track. My fellow-slaves, then, had met with some kindness and some cruelty; but there was, as I have said, one exception to it. Phil. Adams was a strong large man at the time of the wreck, but when I saw him first at Wednoon he was worn away to a shadow, by fatigue and severe treatment, and but for having been sold to the governor's son, who behaved to his people with the greatest humanity, he must have died. I am afraid I cannot recollect all his story, but what I do remember I shall try to give in his own words.

" ' When the fight was over about the plunder of our ship, you remember,' said he to me, ' the stronger party divided us among them. I was given over to two old women, who pushed me on, naked and barefoot as I was, with sticks, till I came up with the remainder of their party, which was at some distance: here I was cruelly used. When I wished for a drink, they made me kneel down, and put my head into the well, like a camel; and when the party set forward, they all rode, except myself. I had to drive on the camels, and keep them together, while the sand through which I walked was so deep that at every step I sank up to my knees. I thought I must have died, the Moors laughing at my distress, and whipping me on the naked back whenever I stopped to take rest. At length they made me mount a camel, and sit behind the hump, to which I was obliged to cling by grasping its long hair with both hands. The heavy motion was to me not unlike that of a small boat in a heavy sea, and its hide was so rough as to take off the skin from my naked thighs and legs, so that the blood trickled down in large drops. When I think of all I endured, it makes me tremble; but I never forgot that my life was in the hand of God, and that the Judge of all the earth would do right.

"'At this rate we continued going until about midnight, when we entered a small valley, and stopped to rest the camels; it seemed the longest and most dismal night I ever passed, for I was in too much pain to sleep. The next day, after the same sufferings, we arrived at the head quarters of the tribe; and here, seeing the miserable state I was in, they indulged me with a covering to sleep under at night. A council was immediately held, at which about one hundred and fifty men were present; they talked over the matter for a long time, seated on the ground, with their legs crossed under them, as a tailor sits at work, and in circles of from ten to twenty each. One of the old men then addressed me; he seemed very intelligent, and though he spoke a language I did not understand, we contrived, by the help of signs, to converse tolerably well. He asked me what country I belonged to. I told him I was English. He then wanted to know how we had come over the sea. I made something to resemble a sea coast by heaping up sand, and forming the shape of a vessel, into which I stuck some sticks, by way of masts, and a bowsprit, and gave him to understand we had been in a large vessel, and wrecked on the coast by a strong wind: then, by tearing down the masts, and covering up the form of the vessel with sand, I signified to him that she had been totally lost. Thirty or forty Moors were sitting around us, assisting the old man to understand me. They asked me if I knew any thing about Marocksh. This sounded something like Morocco. I answered, Yes. Next, of the sooltaan; to which I made signs of assent. I also gave them to understand that I knew him, had seen him with my eyes; and that he was a friend to me and my nation; and if they would carry me to his country, I should get money to pay them for my liberty. They shook their heads; it was a great distance, and nothing for camels to eat or drink on the way. The conference over, I was given to a Moor named Buheri, who brought me to his tent, and made me lie down, like a camel, on the ground. I had eaten nothing that day, but at night he brought me a quart of camel's milk, mixed with water; how delicious I thought it! for sorrow teaches us to value the plenty we have at home. That night I slept soundly, for I was quite worn out with hunger, fatigue, and pain.

" ' At day-light the next day my new master ordered me to drive forward the camels: this I did for about an hour, but my feet were so much swelled and cut by the stones, for I had never before been used to walk barefoot, that at every step I could not help stooping and crouching down nearly to the ground. Seeing this, he stopped the drove, and spreading a piece of blanket behind the camel's hump on which he himself was riding, he made me mount behind him. At night we reached his tents, and found there his wives and children. Two days' rest, which I had here, revived me much; but I was forced to sleep in the open air, his family driving me away with blows, whenever I crept under a corner of their tent. We then set forward for a long journey, as was plain by the preparations they made for it. The face of the country now changed—it was a sandy plain, as level as a lake, with here and there a few thorny bushes, on which the camels fed: these, however, became more scanty, and consequently the camels gave less milk. The provisions with which we had set out, next failed, so that we were soon reduced to great straits. In every valley we came to the natives would run about under every thorn-bush, in hopes of finding some herb, for they were nearly as hungry as myself. In some places a small plant was found, which they tore up and devoured in an instant. I got one or two, but they were very bitter and salt. There was also found by the natives, in particular plains, a small round root, whose top showed itself like a single short spear of grass; they dug it up with a stick; it was of the size of a walnut, and in shape very like an onion; its taste fresh, without any strong flavour; but it was very difficult to find, and was so scarce as to give us but little relief. Some days we found a few dwarf thorn-bushes, not more than two feet high; on these we met with some snails, most of which were dead and dry, but I sometimes got about a handful alive, and used to roast and eat them with great delight.

" ' On one evening, I had an opportunity of observing their devotions. My master, I discovered was a kind of priest, for he was joined by all who happened to be near his tent. The ceremony was as follows:—They washed themselves first with sand, not having any water; then wrapping themselves up in their cloaks, and turning their faces toward the east, my master stepped out before them, and commenced by bowing twice, repeating at each time, " Allah," (the name for God in their language;) then kneeling, and bowing his head twice, he raised himself upon his feet, and repeated a long sentence. He was always accompanied in his motions and words by all present, who could see him distinctly, as he stood before them. He then made a long prayer, and repeated what I supposed to be an exhortation like our sermon, and then all joined in singing some hymn for a considerable time. This ceremony being ended they again bowed themselves, with their faces to the earth, and the service concluded.'

" But I must shorten this story of Phil. Adams, father, for I have still a great deal to tell you. It was about this time that two strangers arrived at his master's tent, riding two camels, loaded with goods; the forms they go through on such occasions are curious. When these travelling merchants come to a camp of Moors, they stop opposite to the tents, and making their camels lie down, seat themselves on the ground, with their faces turned the other way. If the men are abroad, the women go out to them with water, and a roll of tent cloth, to make them a shelter. In the case I mention, the strangers rose as the women drew near, and saluted them with the usual expression, *Peace be with you*, which was returned by the women, who immediately pitched a tent on the spot where they were sitting. They then took the bundles and the camels' harness, with every thing belonging to the strangers, and placed them in this tent. The forms of hospitality being thus attended to, the women seated themselves on the ground, beside their guests, asked them whence they came, what goods they had got, how long they had been on their journey, &c. You see from this, father, that these people, savage as they are, have some good among them. What can be kinder than such a welcome to those whom perhaps they never saw before, and may never meet again. The arrival of these two merchants was a lucky thing for Adams; they bought him from his master, in the expectation of making money by bringing him to Wednoon, where they knew there was a good chance of his being purchased by some European agent. 'No one could have been more particular,' said Adams, 'than they were in endeavouring, as well as they could, to inquire of me whether they were likely to gain by their purchase. They taught me to count in Arabic on my fingers, up to twenty-six, and then asked me did I think I would bring two hundred dollars; at the same time they showed me a dollar, in order to be sure that we understood each other. I told them, in reply, that I did not doubt, if they carried me to a place where there was an English consul, they would receive that sum.'

"Some days after they set out, they reached a place where it was expected a spring would be found; and it shows how well these people must be acquainted with the desert, that though Adams, on his arrival at the very spot, could see no sign of water, in less than an hour they had found it; it was covered with large rocks, about twenty feet high, excepting a narrow, crooked passage, by which a man could go down to it; it contained about twenty gallons of clear sweet water, and there the whole party supplied themselves, for as fast as they emptied the well, more flowed in from another spring. There, Adams told me, he had an opportunity of judging how much a camel can drink at a single draught; he filled a goat skin, which held about four gallons, fifteen times, and all this was drunk by an old camel belonging to his master; it should be mentioned, however, that it had not drunk any thing for twenty days before. How kind is Providence to place such a supply in the midst of a dreary solitary waste!

"It shows, also, how well accustomed these merchants are to travel the desert, that, like seamen, who can see a vessel when no one else would think it in sight, they can distinguish a camel at an amazing distance. One day, Adams's master came up to him suddenly to say he saw a camel, but no one else of the party perceived any thing of the kind for two hours after; at length all saw a camel appearing like a speck in the distance, but they did not reach the travellers, who were with a large drove of camels, till five hours after. Going on for some hours, they found an Arab asleep on the sand, his two camels remaining beside him. There were large sacks lying on the ground, near the sleeping Arab, one of which Adams's master carried off without any ceremony; it was filled with barley meal, and had it been honestly come by, would have been delicious. In half an hour after the owner came running after the party, hallooing to them to stop, but they pushed on the camels the faster: what followed was extraordinary—he gained upon them fast, and when within hearing, made his appeal to them, saying that he had lost part of his property, and knew they must have taken it: that he was their brother, and would rather die than commit such a bad action. 'You have fire arms,' said he, 'and I have but a sword; you believe you can kill me in an instant, but the God of justice is my shield, and will protect the innocent: I do not fear you.' Adams's master upon this told the Arab to leave his sword behind him, and to approach without fear. Upon this he came forward, and asked, 'Is it peace?' 'It is.' 'Peace be to you—peace be to all your house, to all your friends;' and immediately all seated themselves in a circle on the ground, shaking hands in the most cordial manner. 'You would not have refused us a morsel, had you been awake,' said Adams's master, 'for we were in a state of starvation :' the conclusion was, that all the property taken was restored, with the exception of the meal which had been used ; and both sides parted perfect friends."

" Their notions of honesty can't be strict," said farmer Jackson, " if they think that hunger is an excuse for robbery."

" That's true," said Tom ; " but I suppose Adams's master thought it a hard thing to be dying of hunger, when there was plenty lying before him."

" It is all true, Tom ; but what kind of an excuse is that in the sight of Him who is of purer eyes than to behold iniquity ?"

" This was the principal part of what I heard from Adams; for in a short time after he arrived in Wednoon. It was in telling anecdotes to each other in this way that we spent many an hour. Many plans also for gaining our liberty were talked over; but we were too closely guarded to think of making our escape ; and besides, the distance to Mogadore, where there was an English merchant living, took away every hope that we could reach it on foot. We, therefore, resolved to make our case known to our countryman by letter ; and, in order to persuade our masters to send to Wednoon, we told them that they would receive, most probably, a very large sum for our ransom. On this occasion I was the scribe, and, indeed, I made our request as strong as possible, praying him to send some one with power to purchase our liberty, and that our countrymen at home would surely pay him whatever sum he gave. A long time, however, passed before we got an answer, so that all but myself began to despair. I was not so fortunate in a master as my companions, for he treated me with great cruelty; and indeed I have since thought it was from a wish to force me to change my religion, that he acted so. Thank God, I never would consent. My comrades, however, were not so steady, and bitterly they repented of it; as I told you, the moment they became Mohammedans, they were free; each was presented with a horse, a musket, a blanket, and allowed to take a Moorish wife. Think what they must have felt, when three days after they had renounced their religion, a letter came from the English merchant at Mogadore, addressed to the Christian prisoners at Wednoon, exhorting us to resist all attempts to make us give up our religion, and assuring us that within a month we should be set at liberty. Two of them heard the letter read without being much affected, but poor Adams became so moved that he let it drop out of his hands, and burst into tears.

"In about a month the man who brought us the answer, in the disguise of a trader, though in fact he was a servant of our humane countryman, told me he had succeeded in procuring my release; and the next day, after taking a sorrowful farewell of my companions, who appeared doomed to end their days among these Moors, we set out for Mogadore. How shall I speak the joy I felt when I exchanged the jolting step of the camel for the easy step of the mule, which my deliverer sent out to meet me ? It seemed to me a pledge that I was to be no longer a slave to the cruel Moors. The back of this animal, when about to commence a journey, is covered with a large saddle, too broad for a man to bestride, and reaching almost from the head to the tail; over this they place a strong matting, from which hang, on each side, two baskets, something like the turf panniers which horses carry in our neighbourhood. In these they put their provisions, merchandise, and clothing, when on a journey. The rider sits sidewise on the saddle, above the panniers, and rides extremely easy, the mule's gait being a fast ambling walk, which gives very little motion. Indeed, so pleasant did I find it, that I fell fast asleep, and got an ugly fall.

" Our road now lay through a beautiful and fertile country: in one part we passed through a fertile valley, the steep hills on each side being covered with gardens, which rose one above the other. I suppose the rain would have washed all the soil down, if each garden was not kept on a level by means of stone walls, which were filled with rich mould; they were well stocked with all kinds of kitchen vegetables, fig and date trees, and vines, which were reared up the side of each wall, and with melons;

gutters were curiously placed around these gardens, by which the owner could convey water to any part he pleased. At another time we saw a number of small towns, handsomely enclosed with high stone walls; the land on the plain was fenced off into separate fields by rough stone walls, made with great labour. Numerous flocks of goats were feeding on oil nuts, and herds of camels, asses, and horses, were grazing. We met, also, at different distances, large droves of camels, mules, and asses, laden with salt and other merchandise, and driven by a number of Moors; these had each, beside his *haick*, which is a large piece of woollen cloth resembling a blanket, a close jacket next his skin; they wore turbans on their heads, and were armed with daggers and crooked swords, hanging from their necks by red woollen cord. The point of the dagger points inward, like a pruning knife, so that, holding it with the lower part of the hand next the blade, they give what we call a backhanded stroke, ripping open whatever part of the body they strike.

"Our way next led us through a province which had been laid waste by locusts, so that we could procure neither grass nor barley for our horses. These animals are, you know, mentioned in Scripture, and are, indeed, a scourge in these hot climates. Sometimes, I was told, they fly in such swarms as to look like a black cloud in the air; and when they alight, so completely do they cover the ground that it is made to appear alive; it is not surprising, therefore, that in a few minutes, every blade of grass, every leaf on the trees, and, in short, every green thing, should disappear completely, and the whole country, though in the midst of summer, becomes as naked as if it was the depth of winter.

" We next came to a celebrated salt spring, which supplies the entire country with that valuable commodity. The water runs from the side of a hill into a number of shallow earthen pans; where the heat of the sun soon dries it up, leaving a crust of salt at the bottom. It will give you some idea of the trade which is carried on in salt to say that there were not less than five hundred beasts of burden waiting at that time for loads.

" It was during our journey to the place where I expected to gain my liberty, that my guide told me of the hardships sometimes endured by the caravans which cross the desert. You have already heard what I suffered; but what he related to me was so extraordinary, that I don't think I have forgotten a single word.

" When the caravan of which he formed one set out, there were not less than one thousand men and four thousand camels, and it is an extraordinary kind of provision they carry for the camels on this journey. There is a sort of olive called the Argan olive, which grows in Africa; these the natives gather, and after pressing the oil out of them so as to leave them quite dry, they bake them until they are hard, and black as coals; so that some travellers, who were ignorant of this custom, have actually thought, on seeing them, that the camels were eating coals.

"For the first fifteen days they travelled over a level tract of country, where the ground was so hard that not even the track of a camel's foot could be seen on it. In one spot there were a few shrubs which the camels liked of all things to eat of, for, as all the wells they passed by were dry, we may suppose how much they relish a bit of green food after living day after day upon the dry substance that was provided for them. Think what a relief it was to the poor creatures when, after travelling in this way for a fortnight, they came to a fine deep valley, in which they found twenty wells; however, there were only six that had water in them, but these six supplied them with enough to fill the bags, made of skin, which they carry with them for that purpose. In three days more, they came to drifts of very fine loose sand, among which they travelled nearly a week, when there suddenly began to blow a fierce wind from the south-east; this dreadful wind sometimes blows in these deserts, and is called the *simoom;* they could neither advance nor retreat, so they had nothing for it but to take the loading off the camels, and pile it in one great heap, and to make the camels lie down. The dust, or sand, flew so thick that they could not see each other nor their camels, and were scarcely able to breathe; so they lay down with their faces to the ground, and prayed to Almighty God to spare their lives. For two days the wind blew in this dreadful way, and the sand drifted in such a heap on them that they were obliged to move themselves now and then when it became so heavy upon them as almost to suffocate them. It pleased God that many of their lives should be spared; the wind fell, and they ventured to crawl out from beneath the sand which had almost covered them; but when they began to count their numbers, after they had got up, *full three hundred were missing;* they had been stifled in the sand, and were never seen more. All those that survived knelt down, and returned thanks to God for their merciful deliverance;—they then set about digging the unfortunate camels out of the sand, of which two hundred were found dead: this, and reloading those that were able for the journey, took them nearly two days; and after giving the poor animals some drink from the skin bags of water they carried with them, and feeding them on the dried Argan olive, they once more set forward on their journey.

"'There was nothing green to be seen as they travelled along. For twenty-four days they kept on, as fast as they could, through the dry hot sand, so deep that they sank in it at every step; not a bush nor an herb was to be seen, and the camels were dying fast. Both men and animals were sorely distressed with all their sufferings. The principal man in the caravan at length proposed that three hundred of the camels should be killed, to supply food for the men; but this was an unfortunate piece of advice; for just as they were going to put it in execution, a dreadful dispute arose among the owners; some would not let theirs be killed, while others proceeded to seize on them by force; at length they came to open battle; the man who first proposed it was put to death in a moment; and so furious was the combat that between two and three hundred were killed on that day."

"And, Tom, did they succeed in killing the camels, after all?"

"Nothing that's done in a riot ever comes to good: there were more camels destroyed in the fray than would have been killed if the people had been peaceable; there were not less than five hundred put to death, and during the night two of the men set off with thirty-two camels, and upward of twenty of their own friends; and the remainder of the camels died so fast from want of water, and hardship of every kind, that in twelve days afterward, out of the four thousand that had set out, there were but eighteen left alive. At this time the rain set in, and fell in torrents, and they reached a small Negro village built on the borders of the desert. The people flocked around them when they arrived, and treated them with great kindness when they heard of all their sufferings, and saw them come unarmed. Those are a peaceable, harmless people, who live in their own little towns, which they enclosed with fences made of strong reeds, and covered with clay. The travellers stopped a few weeks here, hoping that some of those they had left behind for dead might perhaps yet arrive, but not one of them ever made his appearance.

"But to go on with my own story. We had been now three days and nights almost constantly travelling from Wednoon to Mogadore, when at length my guide called out to me, 'Keep up your spirits only a few hours longer, and you will be in Mogadore, if the Almighty please.' This was at eight o'clock in the morning; at eleven we were mounting a sand hill, over which our path lay, when suddenly the harbour of Mogadore broke upon my view. I earnestly and devoutly returned thanks to Providence for my deliverance; but what was my joy, as I drew nearer, to see a vessel riding at anchor, with English colours flying! My heart beat with violence, and it seemed to me as if I had begun a new life. My generous deliverer also came out to meet me, and appeared so happy that a stranger would have thought that he, and not I, was the person ransomed from slavery. In his house I remained for two months, and received from him such kindness as restored me to health. I had also the opportunity of returning to Europe in the English vessel, but I don't know why, I preferred rambling a little longer. I had an offer to stay in Mogadore, but at the same time a gentleman of the name of Wilson proposed to me to become his servant. He was a man of large fortune, and from a wish to do good to his fellow-creatures, at the same time that he gratified his own thirst for knowledge, he had left all the comforts of home, with the design of travelling over every part of Africa; the wages he was to give me were handsome, and he also promised to make every thing as comfortable as possible. 'I shall have,' said he, 'to endure much myself, and I hope you will not think much of suffering hardship when you see your master no better off than yourself.'

"Accordingly, every thing being agreed on, we set out in a few weeks to travel around by Morocco, and the Barbary states which skirt the Mediterranean, to Egypt. But I should first explain to you, that Africa, which you know is one quarter of the world, is almost surrounded with water. On the north runs the Mediterranean Sea, on the shores of which we were now going to travel; on the west the great Atlantic Ocean washes the whole side, from the Straits of Gibraltar to the Cape of Good Hope, a stretch of above five thousand miles; on the east lie the great Indian Ocean, the Red Sea, and the small gut of land called the Isthmus of Suez, which is about fifty-six miles in length, and joins Africa to Arabia in Asia. When I have told you all my adventures, for I have had the good fortune to visit almost every part of this region, you will understand better what I mean by comparing it to a cloak of frieze bordered with gold lace; the frieze representing the middle parts, of which very little is yet known, as I have told you, and the laced border being the parts which the natives inhabit, and which we know by the accounts of various travellers. In the middle, also, lies that great desert which I have already mentioned, and which but for the camel would be quite impassable. Having set out from Mogadore, on our journey northward, we passed through a rich and fertile country, in which they grow wheat, barley, and maize, and most kinds of kitchen-garden vegetables ; various kinds of fruit trees also, as the date, the fig, the pomegranate, the orange, the olive, and the almond, all which yield great abundance in their seasons : they have also great numbers of camels, horses, asses, mules, oxen, goats, and sheep, so that you might suppose, with such plenty, they are the happiest people on the earth ; it is not so, however; they are ignorant, and ignorance is the parent of every vice ; and they are subjects of a king who is a despotic tyrant: and often, on the slightest cause, will take not only their property, but life. Indeed, if a man makes a little money by industry, he strives to conceal it, for he knows, if it come to the governor's knowledge, he will take it from him by force. How different, thought I, from our country, in which there is the same law for all conditions. The Moors are stout-built, and well-sized ; their colour is tawny ; their dress is a kind of shirt, without sleeves, made of linen or muslin, over which they wear a woollen blanket, called a haick, which I mentioned before. The men shave their heads smooth, and wear turbans. The women live in strict privacy; in the streets they are seldom seen, and then so completely covered that they commonly peep out of a hole left in the front, with one eye; and they are so very fat that they waddle in a most strange manner: indeed, no Moorish lady has any claim to beauty, unless she is so fat as to be almost unwieldy. It was in a place called Tangier, that, some years ago, an English doctor had been sent for to cure the emperor's son, with a promise of a great reward if he succeeded: he was called in, at the same time, to several Moorish ladies of high rank, but it was with great difficulty he could see his patients. The first to whom he was admitted had a curtain drawn quite across the room, through a hole in which she put out her hand, in order that her pulse might be felt. The doctor, anxious to see his patient, told her it was quite necessary he should look at her tongue; upon which, a slit was made in the curtain, that she might put her tongue out, without suffering any other part to be seen. Indeed, he met with the same reserve in all until they found that if they wanted his advice, they must show themselves openly.

" Fez is the capital of Morocco, and the place where the emperor resides: like all other Moorish towns, it has no bells in the places of worship, but there are high steeples, to the top of which their priests mount, at stated times, to call the people to prayers. I was always awakened by them in the morning, and their call used to remind me of *my* duty also."

" Were you ever, Tom, in one of their Moorish chapels ?"

" I assure you I took good care never to see more than the outside of them; for if a Christian enters a Mohammedan place of worship, he must either change his religion, or suffer instant death. I never saw such crowds as in the markets of Fez : for, although it contains no more than one hundred thousand inhabitants, the wandering Arabs resort to it, to buy whatever necessaries they want. The streets are narrow, and the walls of the houses, which are built of earth, have no appearance of windows, except some small holes to look out at ; they are lighted from a square court in the middle of each house, and though the outsides have a very mean appearance, the rooms are handsomely painted, and adorned with gold and silver. Their way of building is curious: they place a large wooden case where the wall is to stand, and into this they put the mortar and stones : when it is dry, they take away the case, and the wall, of course, remains. The houses are generally two stories high; the roofs are flat; and the women, who live always in the upper rooms, walk and pay visits along them.

" When eating, the Moors never use either table or chair ; the dishes are placed on a piece of greasy leather, around which they sit crosslegged on the ground. Their dishes are made of pewter or earthenware, narrow below and wide above, almost like a hat with a high crown.

"On the way through Morocco we met a great number of moveable villages of the Arabs; these people live in tents, and wander from one spot to the other, according as the scarcity of food warns them to shift their ground. Their manners are very singular; they live in families, and will pitch their tents in companies of one hundred, or more, tents. Near sowing time, they encamp beside some spot which they intend to cultivate: they then enclose some fields with good strong fences, and sow the land with wheat, barley, corn, or pease: the sowing thus finished, they remove again, for the sake of finding grazing for their cattle, and wander up and down until harvest time, when they return, and gather in the crops which they have sown. This is generally at the end of August, three months after the sowing of the seed. It is cut about half a foot from the ear, and made up in little bundles; at which work every one labours from morning to night. When the harvest is over they set fire to the long stubble, and do not visit the same spot for two or three years. Their granaries are strangely constructed; they are large holes dug in the ground, and shaped like a beehive turned upside down: when these are filled with corn they are covered with planks placed close to each other, on which earth is laid, level with the ground, to prevent its being discovered by enemies."

"From what you say, Tom, I suppose they

have no men of large estate there, who own a great many acres, and let them to farmers ?"

" No ; the land is there in common, and when they pitch upon any spot, and till it, all the corn they raise from it belongs to the whole tribe. You think this, perhaps, a fine thing; but, if you saw the country they live in, you would own our plan far better ; for their farming is so bad, and they are so fond of that roving life, that they are often in great want, although they might sow as much ground as they please. Give me an acre of ground, even at a smart rent, and a good spade, and I warrant you, with a good pair of arms, able and willing to work, I'll live like a prince, when compared to these Arabs. Look out from your door at the smiling fields ; do you think I ever saw in these outlandish places such a thing as yon field of wheat, or such a fine piece of meadow as that one across the road ? And then to live under a piece of linen always, instead of such a comfortable place as your cabin, and so troubled with vermin and insects that you could not lie down in safety ! No, father, I believe very few would be murmuring about what they have not, if they thought rightly of what they have. When these Arabs wish to shift their encampments, they load all their goods on their camels and oxen, on whose backs they also place their wives and children in large wicker-baskets. A wicked or undutiful child might learn from these barbarians a lesson of love and obedience to his parents. The old always receive the first drink of milk, and when provisions run low they have by far the largest share. On a march, the camel is first prepared for the old man by fixing a basket, in which they carefully place him; and when the tent is pitched at night, he is as carefully taken out the first, and placed under it, in order that he may refresh himself by sleep.

"On our arrival at Morocco, my master was sent for by the emperor, and when he made his visit, he brought me along with him. We found him sitting in an English post-chaise, with his guards drawn up in a half moon behind him He was a very cruel man, often putting his subjects to death for the most trifling cause; indeed, we were told that, when he happened to be in an ill temper, he often cut off the heads of his guards, or attendants, with his own hands. Whenever he wears yellow, it is a sure sign that he will inflict death on some one; for there is no such thing as law in that country. He was very civil, however, to my master; asked him many questions about England, and was so pleased with his answers that he sent him the next day a present, wrapped up in a cloth, by one of his grand officers. From the manner in which it was presented, we thought it must be something very valuable, and could scarcely hide our anxiety to open it till the messenger was gone; but what was our surprise to find nothing but two black loaves. I should be sorry to eat such bread at home; but my master was obliged to conceal his disappointment, every one assuring him that this was the highest mark of regard which the sultan could bestow, and showed that he considered him a brother.

"But although my master thought little of his present, he was very thankful for a letter which came along with it, allowing him to travel through his states, and directing all his subjects to receive him with honour, and send him on his journey, with a sufficient guard for his protection. This enabling us to travel with great safety and comfort through the whole of Morocco, we set out in a few days for Algiers, which is the capital of the next state, and is built on the shore of the Mediterranean. In several of the towns we passed through, we found a house where travellers are lodged and entertained for one night, at the public expense. On the roads, however, we could get no accommodation except when we fell in with a horde of Arabs; these we always found willing to give us shelter and food for one night, and they thought themselves sufficiently paid by a present of a knife, a couple of flints, or a little English gunpowder. When any of their women were particularly kind, my master would compliment them with a pair of scissors, a large needle, or a skein of thread, which they received with a thousand thanks. But we were obliged to wear the dresses of the country, and to appear as merchants; for the Arabs are very jealous of strangers; they think them spies to examine the country, and that they will be followed by an army sent to subdue them, for they have no idea that a man would travel out of mere curiosity. You are surprised that the mere dress should make such an alteration in the appearance of a foreigner as to quiet their suspicions; yet so it is; perhaps, because they imagine that those who put on their peculiar dress have been long settled among them, and have given up every other country but that in which they live. Our road lay across a long chain of high mountains, the sides of which are covered with fruit and forest trees, nearly to the top, except that here and there you see a large rock, on which we found a wretched people no better than savages, living in villages enclosed by a mud wall.

"We arrived at Algiers without accident, and never did I see such a crowded place; it is said to contain above one hundred and twenty thousand inhabitants, and yet I walked around it in about an hour. It stands on the side of a hill fronting the sea, and the houses rise so gradually above each other that, looking at it from the waterside, you see the whole of it. The hills and valleys around the city, however, are beautified with gardens and summer-houses, where the rich live; their dwellings are generally white, and the gardens well stocked with fruit and vegetables. In the desert you know how much I suffered from thirst, but there was no want of water in Algiers; streams of water are constantly flowing down the sides of the hills, and almost in every street you meet with fountains.

"Toward the sea side, Algiers has the strongest fortifications I ever saw; and, indeed, they need all the cannon they can collect, to defend them, for they make war upon almost every nation of Europe, sending out pirate vessels which attack whatever ships they meet with, and make slaves of the crews."

"I wonder, Tom, our own country allows them to rob in this way. I think, if some of our men of war were sent to throw down their batteries, it would be doing a good act. If that was done, they would be obliged to keep quiet; for, when they sit under shelter of the guns, they feel secure, knowing that no small force could attack them."*

"I assure you they often run out of their harbour, and after a short cruise will return perhaps with two or three vessels that they have seized on the opposite coast of Italy. Indeed, I am told their ships crews will sometimes land and carry off the inhabitants to their own country, where they are sold for slaves."

* At the time Tom was in Algiers, the case was exactly as he has stated it; since that, however, the conduct of the Algerines became so bad, that an English fleet was sent against them, which soon brought them to submission. The honour of first humbling the Algerines effectually belongs to the United States of America, which, in 1815, "dictated a treaty to the dey, by which the United States were for ever absolved from paying tribute to these pirates, as they and other Christian nations had formerly done." In 1830, the French sent a strong force against them, subverted their government, and took possession of the city of Algiers, with its dependant towns, which they still retain.

"When so much dishonesty is found in their conduct to strangers, I suppose they cannot be very just in their dealings with each other."

"Indeed it could scarcely be expected: you know the old saying, 'Might is not always right.' The country is ruled by a parcel of soldiers, who always choose the governor out of their own body; and his first act is to put those to death who opposed his election; they rise, therefore, from the ranks, and are not ashamed to acknowledge their humble origin. When I was there the dey had a dispute with the consul of a neighbouring state, in the course of which he acknowledged, that he had once been a private soldier: 'My mother,' said he, 'sold sheep's feet, and my father neat's tongues, but they would have been ashamed to bring to market such a worthless tongue as thine!' You must not suppose, however, that this governor, who had been raised from the lowest to the highest station, is thereby made happy; it were better for him, by far, if his parents were poor, to have continued so himself, for scarcely one in ten of their governors dies a natural death.

"When the Algerines dine, they sit cross-legged around a table about four inches high, and use neither knives nor forks. Before they begin, they say, 'In the name of God;' and when the meal is over, a slave pours water over their hands. Sherbet and coffee are their usual drink, wine being forbidden by their religion. They are for the most part fair: the rich suffer their beards to grow, and wear clothes of most costly materials; the ladies colour their eyebrows with lead, which gives them a very strange appearance.

"When a person dies, the corpse is carried to the grave attended by a great crowd; the funeral proceeds not slowly, as with us, but as fast as they can carry it, the persons present singing some verses out of the Koran, which is the book that contains the doctrines of their religion; the female relations, for two or three months after, visit the grave once a week, at the head and foot of which, upright stones are placed, and the space between is either planted with flowers or paved with tiles.

"The contract of marriage is settled always by the parents; the young people being united without ever having known each other before, and the only ceremony is drinking out of each other's hands. The fathers agree upon the sum that is to be settled on the lady, as also on the present she is to receive.

"Tunis, the next city on the coast which my master arrived at, stands, like Algiers, on a rising ground, along the western bank of a large lake; it is surrounded by marshes, which would probably make it very unhealthy, if it were not for the salubrity of the climate and the abundance of sweet-smelling plants which grows there; indeed, so plentiful are they, that the people gather them for fuel to heat their ovens and baths. The town is not so large as Algiers. The people are fearless, ignorant, and savage.

"In the kingdom of Tunis, the rich entertain their friends on certain occasions, such as a marriage feast, with the honey of the palm tree, which is thought a great delicacy, and well it may, for, in order to get it, the whole tree is destroyed. They cut off the head or crown, and scoop the top into the shape of a bowl, into which the sap rises, and for nearly the first fortnight it yields three or four quarts a day; after this, however, the tree is good for nothing but for timber or firewood; the liquor is sweeter than honey, and, when kept till it grows tart, makes a strong spirit by being distilled. There is also a tree, the leaves of which are made use of by the African women for dying their lips, hair, hands, and feet, of a saffron colour, which they think greatly adds to their beauty."

"That appears to us very absurd, Tom; yet I warrant they would think our ladies just as foolish for painting their cheeks and eyebrows, as I am told some do—but I suppose they don't spend so long a time decking themselves," continued old Jackson, "as some in this country?"

"I don't know as to that," answered Tom, "but when a lady of rank is dressing, she has a number of women slaves about her, each of whom has a different employment: one plaits the hair, another perfumes it, a third settles the eyebrows, and a fourth paints the face; in short, the full dress employs several hours, and alters her appearance so much that her nearest relations can scarcely know her.

"I don't think it necessary to say much of Tripoli, which is the next town on the coast, going east, and very like those I have already mentioned; we arrived there just at the time the plague was raging, and of course passed through it as quickly as possible. It had made great ravages, my master was informed, before they took any means of checking it. On such occasions, it is always the custom for the Europeans who reside there to shut themselves up within their houses, and to hold no communication with the people, for fear of taking the infection, but at the request of the governor they did not do it at first, for fear of creating an alarm. The deaths, however, grew more numerous, and they were obliged to adopt it. At such times no native is admitted into their houses, unless at one particular time of the day, when a person, hired for the purpose, comes and places provisions on the lobby, with an account of the value, and immediately goes away; on his next visit he finds the sum he had laid out. The plague at length raged so violently that the funerals could not be conducted with any order; the military went once a day around for the dead, and carried them to a common burial place, where they were all placed together, without any distinction. Would you believe that one-third of the inhabitants died?"

"Is it because these people have no doctors among them?" said old Jackson.

"My master said it was partly from want of proper advice, but he believed the principal cause was want of cleanliness. 'I will not say that dirt actually brings sickness,' said my master, 'but of this I am sure, that when fever prevails, it finds no difficulty in seizing on those who have neglected that necessary study, cleanliness; it finds the door of the cleanly closed, but that of the lazy and untidy more than half open to let it in.'

"On our way eastward we crossed a river, about which my master made many inquiries. He told me he had read in a history, that about two thousand years ago, a serpent, one hundred and twenty feet long, disputed the passage with the whole Roman army, killing a great many soldiers; nor was it conquered till the general threw great stones at it with machines, which crushed it. We now entered on the desert of Barca, which divides the state of Tripoli from Egypt, and a dreary waste we found it, almost without water or vegetation.

"Hunting the ostrich is a favourite diversion among the Arabs, who live scattered through this desert. You sometimes see ostrich feathers in ladies' bonnets—you know they are long, flat, and generally of a pure white; the bird which gives them is the tallest of the feathered race, often measuring seven feet from the top of the head to the ground. We met, one day, a party of Arabs in chase of one of these birds; there were not less than twenty, riding at about three-quarters of a mile's distance behind each other. The ostrich never flies, its wings being too short, but it uses them to assist its pace in running, spreading them out wide as it proceeds. When it runs against the wind, however, its wings, if extended, would rather retard its flight, and this is the reason why the hunters get the animal to the windward. As soon as they perceive their prey, they rush upon it in full speed, upon which the ostrich sets off, endeavouring, if possible, to get the wind behind him.

"Soon fatigued, however, it slackens its speed, and is knocked down by the short sticks of those that follow. As soon as those I saw engaged in the pursuit had the bird completely in their power, they proceeded to kill and pluck out its feathers; the spoil was then divided, and a share being given to each of the hunters, they separated, every man going to his home, that he might prepare the food for his family. My master informed me, that when they are obliged to hunt the ostrich with the wind, the silly animal, from its extraordinary swiftness, would soon escape, if instead of going off in a straight line, he did not move in circles, which enables the hunters still to keep him in view, till he becomes quite spent with fatigue: he now finds all escape impossible, and endeavours to hide himself from his enemies by covering his head up with the sand, or in the first thicket he meets.

"'This, father, was all we saw worth remarking, on our journey from Morocco along the shore of the Mediterranean Sea. We were now drawing near to Egypt, of which we read so much in the Bible; and, I confess, I had a great desire to see the country where Joseph had showed himself such an affectionate son, and so kind a brother. I called to mind, that it was here Pharaoh kept the children of Israel in slavery for four hundred years, and that it was upon the banks of the river Nile, which flows through this country, that Moses was found by the king's daughter when his mother had concealed him among the rushes that grew there. It was, therefore, with no small pleasure that, a few days after quitting Tripoli, we entered the city of Alexandria, which lies at the mouth of the Nile, where that river runs into the Mediterranean Sea. Here we stopped but a day or two, as my master was anxious to hasten on to Cairo.

"Alexandria was once a great city, but it is now falling into ruin; and it was a pity to see the beautiful pillars, and the remains of great buildings, all lying broken and decaying on the ground. There are two obelisks still standing, which, they told me, were called Cleopatra's Needles. I cannot forget the name, for sure such needles never were seen: they are each a single block of stone, sixty-three feet high; and there is another fine pillar, called Pompey's Pillar, also made out of a single block of granite, and about the same height. In this country we have no idea of making a pillar out of one great piece of rock; but they had, in those days, the art of cutting those large stones out of the quarry, and of setting them to stand upright. The city is enclosed with great walls, in some places forty, and nowhere less than twenty feet high, around which are one hundred towers, the whole making a circuit of about six miles. The first night I was there, I was awakened with a noise in the town, like a yell, or a kind of bark, of some wild animal, which never ceased till toward dawn of day. Upon inquiring in the morning, I was told that it was the cries of the jackals, who, during the night, collect about the streets in search of food.

"I told you that all the old part of the town is falling into ruins; there is, however, one new street of handsome houses, and inhabited by merchants. This was once a place of great trade, and very wealthy; but war, joined with the indolent habits of the people, has brought it into ruin. The houses are white, and flat-roofed, and the windows not of glass, like ours, but made of a kind of lattice work, sometimes of fine wire bars, sometimes of wood. In hot countries, this kind of window is preferred, because it admits the air. It was curious to see the mixture of different nations, of which the inhabitants of this town are composed; Jews, Turks, Arabians, &c. Their tone of voice is so loud that they almost seem to be bawling at each other, and they have a swinging way of walking, more like running than any thing else. Altogether, I thought they were the oddest looking set of people I ever saw in my life; many a time my master had to caution me, not to let them see me laughing at them, for fear they should be offended : and one day he said to me, what I never thought of before, that, if one of them was to come among us, he would think us just as strange a people as we think them.

"About twelve miles from Alexandria are the ruins of a fine city, called Aboukir, where Lord Nelson won one of his greatest victories. This place is all in ruins, and very poor; there is not a wealthy person in the whole town; every one is obliged to follow some poor trade for his subsistence:—most of the men are fishermen; the governor is a barber, and the person who is next in rank to him in the town is an old Jew, who lives upon a salary of about seven cents a day.

"About six miles from Aboukir we crossed a ferry, called Medea : from Medea our road lay through very dry sand; to avoid which, my master and I rode in the sea, along by the edge of the sand; we then took the shore again, and pursued our road eastward. Here we observed small brick towers, eleven of them placed at equal distances, I suppose to mark out the way for travellers, as this was all a stretch of sand, and, of course, no regular road made through it. At length we came to Rosetta, and glad enough were we to reach it, though one has but little comfort in arriving at the end of a journey in these countries ; the towns are so dirty, and the streets so narrrow, that you feel as if you had scarcely air enough to breathe ; there is not a street in Rosetta more than two yards wide : I could touch the shops on each side, when I stretched out my arms, as I walked along.— Having heard that there was to be a public feast in a neighbouring village the next day, my master told me he would be there himself to see it, and that I might attend with him if I pleased.

"When we arrived at the house where the entertainment was given, we found, according to the custom of the country, all kinds of food spread out on the carpet upon the floor: there were immense dishes of rice, either boiled in milk or made into a kind of soup. I saw several half sheep and quarters of lamb roasted, as also the heads of different animals boiled, vegetables, jellies, sweetmeats, creams, honey in the comb, and large loaves of bread. The water for drink was served about in a large jar, and the chief man of the village, who had given the feast, took the first draught of the water, and was the first to taste the different dishes. During dinner, I remarked that the company wiped their hands and lips with a slice of bread; however, after dinner, the attendants brought bowls of water and napkins, and each person washed his hands, and then began to smoke and drink coffee. They were going to begin their feast when my master and I went in; they received us kindly, and when I saw my master seated, I was just going to place myself at the lower end of the room, (for table they had none, every thing was laid out upon the floor,) but he made a sign to me not to do so; I therefore stood behind him, to wait on him during the feast, and he then told me that all the attendants were to dine after their masters, and that of course I should wait till it came to my turn. But, indeed, I was not thinking much of eating, I was so entertained with the strange sights before me. However, there was a quantity of food laid out, and when these had finished, all the respectable poor people of the village came in, and sat down to eat; after them came some persons poorer still than they. I remember one poor beggar, who humbly begged to get a morsel; and as at these public feasts it is reckoned sinful to turn away any person without letting him have his share, he was readily admitted. Next came our turn, and though you might think, after so many had eaten before us, but little would remain, yet, I assure you, such was the quantity of provision first laid down, that there was enough left, even after us, for a number of poor strangers, and others who had not yet had their turn, to come in and eat, and who afterward divided among themselves the remains of the feast.

"There are people of almost every nation in the world living in Egypt; and during our stay in the different towns, it was an amusement to us to distinguish them by their various kinds of dress. There was one race of people, in particular, who came from a part of Africa called Nubia, and whose appearance is very singular, their skin being of a shining jetty black, not like any of the blacks I had ever seen, their eyes sparkling, and with bushy black eye-brows; and when the men grow old, their beard becomes white as flax, which, on their black faces, gives them the oddest appearance in the world. They dress themselves in a large woollen cloth wrapped around them, and such as are poor are very humble, work hard, and live sparingly. I was told, also, that those who are servants are the most faithful creatures to their masters; and indeed when I heard it I thought what a shame it was for us Christians, that there should be more virtue found among these poor ignorant people than among many of the servants of our own country, who are well paid and well fed.

"There are also a great many Jews and Turks living in different parts of Egypt."

"Ay, Tom, I should like to hear about the Turks; they are not an industrious hard-working people, like the poor Nubians?"

"I believe," replied Tom, "the Turks are the laziest people in the world: they will sit for the whole day under a shady tree, or on a cushion in the room, smoking tobacco and drinking coffee; those who are rich have their pipes made of fine sweet-scented wood, and I often saw them set with jewels; and they carry their tobacco, which is of the finest kind, in beautiful embroidered silk purses hung from their waists."

"And pray what sort of dress do they wear, Tom?"

"They wear very long robes, which sweep the ground after them as they walk; gloves which reach nearly half a foot beyond the ends of their fingers; and a large head-dress, called a turban, made of a fine piece of silk, wrapped around and around their head, and this is so large and weighty that they are obliged to walk quite straight, and not to stoop, lest it should fall. I believe it is from this early custom of holding themselves so upright, that they all have such a stately air, even to the poorest of them. As I before observed, they are a lazy, indolent people; even those who are obliged to work for their bread will choose such trades as give them least labour, and at these trades they will sit down as much as possible while doing their work. I often thought what good it would do them to be obliged to follow the plough from six in the morning until six in the evening, as we do in this country, earning our bread; for honest industry is the life of us all; and these fellows always seemed to me to be dying for want of some hard work to do.

"The Egyptian women wear long veils of thick black cloth, with two holes cut in them for eyes, and take great pains to hide the rest of the face: their eyes are generally fine brown, and they will sometimes die their eyebrows and eye-lashes to make them appear darker.

"The river Nile, which I mentioned to you as flowing through this country, is said to be one of the largest in the world. At a particular time in the year, torrents of rain swell all the mountain streams that fall into it, and cause it to overflow its banks. You may conceive in what quantities it comes down when I tell you that it runs a length of two thousand miles before it discharges itself into the sea. The time of this rising of the river was not while we were there.; but the people of Alexandria told me that at those times the whole face of the country around is covered with water; nothing is then to be seen but trees and houses, which, in this part of Egypt, are always built on little hillocks, which raise them up out of the water, so that a person looking out from one of these hills, it would seem as if there was nothing but one great sea before him, with a few scattered trees and houses standing up through it.

"This watering is of great use to the soil, and is doubtless sent by Providence to supply the want of rain, which in this country seldom falls. The houses of all the small villages in Egypt, and the poor people's cottages, are built of mud, and have generally but one room. The peasantry of Egypt live very poorly; their principal food is a cake made of a kind of Indian corn; this, with a drink of water, and a few onions, is what they usually live upon; it is only the more wealthy who can afford themselves a little cheese, sour milk, honey, or a few dates, a fruit as common there as apples with us. After a few days at Rosetta, we sailed up the river Nile to Cairo. It surprised me to see how close the villages were built to each other all along the banks: in the space of twelve miles I counted fifteen on one side only. The country is fertile and well cultivated.

" And what kind of grain do they grow there, Tom ?" said his father.

" Principally Indian wheat and rice, and a good deal of Indian millet : this is the grain of which the poor people make their cake bread.

" The city of Cairo stands nearly on the banks of the river Nile, and every house has a garden to it. The streets are exceedingly crowded; and it surprised me to see what numbers of camels, mules, and asses they have in use there. Their asses are large fine looking animals : their step is light and brisk, and they are very sure-footed; they are taken very good care of, especially by the rich, who prefer them to horses for long journeys, because they are better able to bear hard labour, and do not require either as good food or as much as a horse would. There were also vast numbers of goats in Cairo ; I have seen them driven in flocks through the town, and the owners milking them in the streets, and selling the milk to the passengers, who, in this hot country, willingly pay for a good drink.

" The people suffer greatly in Egypt, and more particularly at Cairo, from a bad disorder in their eyes, called ophthalmy, which is common to the country. Many persons are quite blind, and almost every one suffers from it more or less: of one hundred whom I met in the streets, twenty were totally blind, ten had but one eye, and twenty at least had their eyes bleared. I believe all Egyptians are indolent, but at Cairo they appear as though they would rather let their houses fall down about them, than take the trouble of repairing them."

" Well, Tom, I think if people were ever so lazy, the comfort of a good house is the last they would part with."

" Indeed, so one would think, father; but in these warm countries, and where there is so little rain, they don't mind it as much as we should. I assure you, I have seen that when the wall of a house in Cairo was out of repair, and threatening to fall, they would just prop it up, and when it had partly fallen, they laid out their furniture in the open space, and continued to live there till the house fell down entirely, when they left it there in ruin, and went off to settle themselves in another.

" There is a great canal running through the town, which, when the Nile rises, is supplied with water from that river; at other times it is quite dry, and serves as a public receptacle for all kinds of offal. Until the Nile has risen to its greatest height, a high bank of earth is drawn across the end of the canal, and the channel is cleared; and when the stream has risen to a proper height, this bank is removed, and the water flows rapidly into the canal up through the town, and though a number of smaller channels to the more distant fields. This is the time for all kinds of gayety at Cairo: barges and small boats, crowded with company, are to be seen in great numbers on the water in the evening, many of them with bands of music on board; the houses are illuminated, the windows filled with company, and a quantity of fireworks are thrown up from the town. This takes place during the month of August. As soon as the waters begin to decline, the canal in time gets dry, and they sow corn in its bed, so that shortly after, in the spot where there was nothing to be seen but one sheet of water, we find the corn in full growth.

"The Egyptian horses are as beautiful as the Arabian, although they have not such great strength, but they are finely shaped, and very spirited, and yet so gentle that any one could guide them. They walk remarkably well, never trot, but gallop with great speed, and can stop short in a minute.

"The great men of Cairo generally keep from fifty to two hundred horses, fifty or sixty slaves, and as many servants, besides other attendants.

"I followed a funeral one morning at Cairo; the body was carried on a bier, the priests walked before, repeating aloud sentences from a religious book, and many women followed, mourning, and uttering cries of grief. All the burial grounds are outside of the town: when they have laid the body in the grave, they set up a small pillar of stone at the head, with a turban on the top of it; and it is usual for the friends of the deceased to visit the grave every Friday for a considerable time after.

"There is a considerable manufactory of linen at Cairo, made of the fine flax of Egypt But I should tell you of the manner in which chickens are hatched at Cairo. The people heat large ovens, as nearly as possible to the same degree of warmth that the hen gives to eggs by sitting upon them: into this oven they will put seven or eight thousand eggs, which in two and twenty days are hatched. This process is repeated for four months, and during that time some hundred thousand chickens are produced. Those engaged in this business make a good livelihood by going through the country in the proper season; and though, to be sure, the eggs sometimes fail, as perhaps by thunder, which injures them very much, or by some accident, yet what I have said proves that this art is pursued with wonderful success.

"The day after we arrived at Cairo, my master hired two horses, and made me accompany him out of the town, about twelve miles, to the village of Gize, to see what are called the pyramids of Egypt, which used to be called one of the seven wonders of the world. There are several of them, and they are all built in the same form, square at the bottom, and gradually growing narrower, until they come almost to a point at the top. Each side of the great pyramid is seven hundred feet long at the base, and the building is of such vast size that the top appears almost a point in comparison with it, although it is sixty feet square. They are made of a kind of white stone, called freestone; and this one, which I have described, is six hundred feet high. In order to bring the building narrow to the top, the stones are not set even one over the other, for then the walls would rise straight up, just like the side of a house; but they are laid one farther in than another, in regular rows or courses all around, so as to leave a ledge of the under stones projecting, which serve as steps for climbing them. It is curious from a distance to see a number of men clambering, step after step, up the sides of this huge building, looking no bigger than so many mice going up a mountain; and I heard that when the British soldiers were there they continually went up and down, without the least accident. Such a quantity of stones did it take to build these pyramids, that I was told, if the largest of them was pulled down, it would furnish enough to build a wall four hundred and fifty miles long, and three feet high."

" And what were these great buildings raised for, Tom? One would think that so much money as they must have cost would not have been expended but for some useful purpose."

" That was the first question I asked my master," said Tom, " and he told me they were built for burial places for the old kings of Egypt. I could not help thinking what a perishable thing the human body is, and how vain it was to raise those great piles of building over what was as insensible to all this grandeur as the stones they were building with.

" I longed of all things to get inside, and my master told me I might accompany him if I pleased. Indeed, he was always very kind to me in this respect, and as ready to answer my questions as if I were his equal in station;

perhaps that might be because he had no other companion. The opening by which we got into the pyramid that we entered is nearly sixty feet from the ground; but it is easily reached by a high mound of sand and rubbish which lies beneath it. We had two Arabs with us as guides, and when we arrived at the entrance, one of them fired a pistol, to frighten away the bats, which collect in great numbers, and build their nests in the inside of the pyramids. Before entering, we were obliged to throw off our clothes, on account of the great heat which is felt within, and each of us carried a lighted wax candle in our hands, for torches would have caused too much smoke in the narrow passages by which we entered. We thought the first narrow enough, indeed, but when we came to the second, it was only two feet wide, and not more than one and a half high; so that we were obliged to lie down on our backs, while the guides took hold of our feet, and dragged us along. This passage was a steep ascent, and was, I should judge, about seven or eight yards long; it led into another gallery, or passage, like the first, and beyond that we found an open space, like a room, where we were so tired that we were glad to stop and take some refreshments. We had then to go through another passage, and thence to descend down a narrow deep hole, which we were obliged to go through just as a chimney sweeper gets down a chimney: this brought us to another chamber, where lay a coffin, made of a single block of granite stone, and which, when one of the guides struck it, sounded quite hollow. And this was all we had gone through such labour and difficulty to see! and it was to contain this single coffin and the lifeless body of some king, whose very name is unknown to us, that all this great pile of building was raised! For my part, I was quite disappointed; but my master examined the coffin, picked up a fragment of the stone off the ground, and showed me how the walls of the chamber had once been white as marble, but were now become quite black from the smoke of the torches which travellers use in visiting this place. We had used only wax lights in going through the narrow passages, but when we came to the coffin chamber, they lighted the torches, and put them out again on quitting it. We returned by the same way we came; but, before we came away, one of the Arabs fired a pistol, which rang through the building like thunder. All the passages are lined with white marble, and so polished that were it not for little holes cut in the floor, for resting the feet in as you walk along, they would be quite impassable.

" When we at length got out, and had put on our clothes, in order to prevent our catching cold, my master proposed that we should ascend up to the top of the pyramid on the outside; we accordingly clambered up, not by the side of the building, but at one of the corners, making our way by stepping up from stone to stone, and always looking out for the safest footing; we reached the top, and so great was the view from it, that I could have thought I was looking over whole countries. We here also amused ourselves reading the names of travellers who had visited this place, and who had cut their names in the stone. Something came across my mind, that some of my old ship companions might, perhaps, be brought here by, chance, as I was myself, and that I might thus let them know I was still in the land of the living, I just took out my penknife, and whoever goes to the top of that pyramid may see the name, " Tom Jackson, of the Caledonia," cut in one of the stones there."

" Now, Thomas, how long did they say it was in building, and where was the money got which paid all the workmen?"

" Why, as to the time they were building it, I was told it took many years; but I don't think it cost much money. In those days, it is said, every third man in all Egypt was forced to give his labour in hewing and carrying the stones to the spot, and this without any wages; but it is the same thing still; these great men can call out the poor to work for them; and if a man dares to murmur, they think no more of taking off his head than I should of striking the ground with my stick. How different from our own happy country, where the laws are made equally for both poor and rich! I should tell you that the entire outside stone-work of the pyramids is all done without mortar, or any thing to keep the stones together; but their own weight, and their all being fitted each to the other, makes them immoveably firm. In all the inside masonry, a great deal of mortar is used, made of lime and clay. It is not long since a great chief in Egypt, having the idea that there was some rich treasure concealed in one of the pyramids that had never yet been opened, employed several hundred workmen to break a passage into the centre of it: for several months the work went on, but the labour was so excessive, and the quantity of rubbish to be cleared away so enormous, that he was obliged to give up the hopes of making himself rich in this way. Of a clear morning, the pyramids can be seen nearly thirty miles off, and look like high white rocks standing up into the clouds. Yet though they look so high at a distance, it is only when you come near to them that you can have a just idea of their amazing size, in every way. They are like a mountain of building; I don't know what else to compare them to.

"Near the foot of the pyramid which we were in is an immense stone figure, called a sphynx, having the head and face of a female, and the rest of the body like that of a lion. It is cut in one piece out of the solid rock, and those which have been thought joinings of the stones, are only veins in the rock. At present, only the head and neck of the figure are above ground, together with the top of the back, to the tail, the rest being covered by the sand, which is here continually drifting; the figure is one hundred and thirty-three feet in length, from the fore part of the neck to the tail, so you may judge what a size it is; the whole head looked almost as big as this cottage; the chin alone is ten feet and a half long, and the face measures sixteen feet in length. I asked my master for what purpose it was made; but he told me that it is not at all known, nor at what time it was done, but that it is supposed to have been formed at the same time with the pyramids. I have told you it took a great many years to build one of those pyramids; but besides that, it took ten years to make the road, and convey the stones to it, and ten more to form the inside of it in the manner I have described to you.

"Having thus satisfied our curiosity, my master and I embarked in a boat he hired, and sailed up the river: at night we landed, and slept at a monastery which stood near the left bank. The monks at first were very unwilling to admit us, being strangers; and though the promise of a handsome present softened them a little, they positively refused to open their gate, but said that if we would let ourselves be drawn up by a rope, they would take us in by one of the upper windows. This, I afterward understood, was done only for their own security, as they lived in great fear of attacks from the wandering tribes of Arabs, who subsist by plunder. The Arabs will sometimes come in a body, and lay siege to a monastery, obliging the monks to furnish them both with provisions and money. I have already mentioned what I know of the habits of these Arabs;

they live in tents, have no fixed place of residence, and change it as often as the scarcity of food compels them to it. Their food is simply milk and dates, or a coarse kind of cake bread; and yet, poor as they are, they never turn away their face from a stranger, or from one that wants relief. There is not a poor traveller who asks leave to rest himself, that would not be made welcome, and given a share of whatever they had. I remember, one day I was present when an Arab sat at his tent door, according to custom, with his food before him; he saw a stranger drawing near; he did not know the traveller, and yet he invited him, with the greatest cordiality, to take share of his hospitality. They ate together, and, after the meal was over, the guest stood up, and said, in a very devout tone of voice, " God be praised ;" an example, though it came from a savage, that I wish all Christians would follow. But to tell you about the monastery:—This was a very strong-built house, in which a number of religious people lived together, and it had a small garden, in which they raised kitchen vegetables for their own use. When they found we had come peaceably, and that no one else was with us, they opened their door, and let us in, and we sat down with them to the meal they had prepared for themselves,—some hard biscuit, rice boiled in salt and water, and a little honey."

" And why, Tom, did your master prefer going there to stopping in the town with the rest of the boat's crew ?"

"The abbot of this monastery, who was at Cairo, had given my master a letter of introduction to these monks, recommending him to their protection, and requesting them to give him whatever advice or assistance was in their power,—and my master, being a stranger in the country, wished to profit by it. We, however, did not make any stay with them, but quitted the monastery at an early hour the next morning; the monks giving us such advice and direction as we stood in need of. As we passed up the river, we often observed the manner in which the inhabitants draw water from it. The women come down with three jars each, and will carry home one very large one on the head, with a smaller one slung on the back by a rope which passes around their forehead; and a smaller still on the left shoulder, held by the right hand. Both men and women are industrious, and labour hard for a poor livelihood. Resting places for travellers are to be seen for a considerable way along the river, southward of the town of Siout, and distant from each other about a mile and a half; they have been built by pious and charitable persons, and consist generally of two chambers, a fountain, a cistern, and a watering trough; and here the traveller may rest, and draw abundance of water for his camels.

"From Siout we continued to sail up the river till we came to Girgeh; here we met a Nubian prince, brother to the king of Darfur, a province in that part of Africa called Nubia.

This was a lively, gay, and clever young man, and, like the Nubians I have already described to you, of an uncommonly black colour. He told us he was going to Cairo, and that he was bringing there a quantity of gold dust and elephants' teeth, which, you know, is what we call ivory and these he was to barter for coffee, sugar, lead, iron, cloth, and shawls, and also for tamarinds, which are a very common fruit in Egypt. These articles, to my great surprise, I found had been brought from Tombuctoo, whence, although it is full six months' journey from Darfur, the inhabitants will come every year, and purchase the articles brought from Cairo, giving gold dust in exchange, for which the merchant is always sure to find a ready sale. This will give you an idea of the manner in which these people carry on trade with each other.

"One night that we slept at a village called Furshout, the chief of a neighbouring town seized on our boat, and detained it for his own use. My master had met, in the village, a merchant, whom he had known at Cairo, and to him he applied in the morning, to know what he should do to recover it. He advised him to apply to an Arab prince, who lived near the town, and to whom he conducted us. The prince was seated under an orange tree in his garden, but stood up, and received my master with great civility; he gave us all some fine grapes and a drink of lemonade, and immediately sent orders for the release of the boat, which was accordingly restored. My master made him a present of some bottles of liquors and Cairo brandy, which were received as a great favour by the chief, who gave him in return letters of introduction to several Arab sheiks, or chiefs, besides ordering a supply of provisions to be sent on board our boat.

" Our next town, of any note, was Dendera. Near this we saw hundreds of crocodiles, an animal common in Egypt. They live in the water, and are said to be very ferocious, but I never knew an instance of their injuring any person. I often bathed in the Nile when the water was full of them, and they never attempted to hurt me.

" The Egyptians sow their grain much in the same way that we plant potatoes; the sower follows the plough, scattering in the furrows just as much seed as is necessary, and this is covered by the plough in opening the next furrow, so that not a single grain is lost.

" The rams of Egypt are large, and have a thick fleece like our sheep; their skins are used for beds by the Egyptians. One of these skins, large enough to serve a man as a mattress, will sell for the value of twenty shillings; while, if the animal was shorn, the owner would not get more than six for him.

" We continued sailing up the river every day, stopping only at such places as my master found any thing worth remarking for, until, at length, we came to the city of Thebes; and here there was enough to induce any one, even me, to stop. Of all the cities I ever saw, and I have now seen a great many, this had the appearance of having once been the finest in the world, though now gone to ruin; and at every step we made, there lay enough to convince us that there is no work of man, however great, but time can destroy. It would grieve you to see all the fine pillars, temples, and obelisks broken and decaying, not indeed *on* the ground, but *in* it; for the earth has collected over them to such a depth that many of the statues are sunk in it up to the waist; and my master told me, that if we were to dig around any of the pillars, we should find it sunk, perhaps, to the depth of twenty or thirty feet; for which reason, though they are of a prodigious size, some of them from nine to twelve feet in thickness, they do not appear of any great height." "I suppose, Tom, the statues are all just the natural size, as large as life." "Ay, father, they are ten times as large; one I cannot forget, which, though half sunk under the earth, stood full thirteen feet above ground, up to the top of a high cap that was upon the head. I heard my master say, that, if well proportioned, the whole figure must be fifty feet in height; so I may well call them nearly ten times as large as a common-sized man.

"We stayed some days at Thebes; for my part, I soon got tired of such a desolate place, for there is scarcely a human being to be seen there, and those few live in the poor huts which are scattered through the town.

"We lodged in an old ill-built house, with mud walls: the night before we came away, the rats were running about in such numbers that it was impossible to sleep: we lay upon the floor, stretched on carpets, my master at one end of the room, and I at the other; and these animals, which are a great deal larger than those of our country, were running over us; and gnawing our carpets, during the whole night. I flung my shoes at them, and every thing else I could reach, but nothing would drive them away, until at length we were driven out ourselves; for it blew a violent storm, and every now and then lumps of clay would break down from the walls of our crazy old house, and at length one of them fairly gave way: fortunately it fell outward, so it did us no hurt; but my master and I sprang up, as did all the people of the house, and made the best of our way out, passing the rest of the night in the open air.

"The inhabitants generally build their houses within the walls of the ruined buildings, and it has a strange appearance to see such poor mud cottages supported against the walls of these magnificent temples and palaces.

"As we stopped at the different towns on our way up the river, my master very often paid a visit to the sheik, or chief governor of the place, and he usually allowed me to attend him. A few days after we left Thebes, we were, for a day or two, at the town of Edfore, and went to wait upon the sheik. My master had a letter of introduction to him, which he received very graciously, read it, kissed it, and put it to his forehead as a mark of respect. My master made him a handsome present, according to the usual custom, and then requested his protection, while he visited the ruins of a fine temple which is near the town. The sheik put his hand to his forehead, signifying, 'Your safety be upon my head,' and then accompanied us to the temple. Here a circumstance occurred which showed us what a regard these people have for their word. A number of persons having assembled around us, while I was standing in the crowd a young lad snatched out of my hand a book I was carrying, and ran away with it. I was going to fly after him, but my master forbade me, fearing lest we should get into a quarrel, by interfering about it; the sheik, however, saw what had happened, threw off his long robe, and ran after the young man, as fast as he could, but did not overtake him, which I am sure was fortunate, for they all said he would have killed him, if he had caught him, though he was his own nephew. However, the story is but trifling, and would not be worth telling, only that in the evening my master was informed he should have back his book, if he would pay a certain sum of money for it, about five shillings. Glad to get it, even on these conditions, he readily gave it, and received the book. The next morning, when we were some hours on our journey, we were followed by a son of the sheik, who told us his father had just learned

Africa.

Egyptian Temple

p. 111

that we had been obliged to pay for the book; that he was extremely indignant that a stranger, to whom he had promised his protection, should have been so ill treated, and he therefore begged of my master to accept of his money back again; wished him a safe journey, and sent him a letter of introduction to a neighbouring sheik. We had travelled many hundred miles, and might travel as many more, without meeting with such an instance of true honesty. And as my master said to me, there was something so upright in it that it might well give a lesson even to the wisest and the best of us. Indeed he was always ready to give me a word of advice; and often told me how much it was in our power to improve ourselves by trying to avoid the faults we see in others. 'Why, sir,' said I, 'when I see good in other people, I would try to follow it myself.' 'Yes,' says he, 'and when you see faults in others, can't you also try to avoid them yourself? One is just as easy as the other, and both are equally our duty.'

"But to go on with my story. You will observe we were not now travelling by water; the town which we had just left was three miles from the shore, on the east side of the river;— our good sheik had provided us with camels, and every thing necessary to our journey, as my master's intention was to proceed for some miles along that side of the river, and then cross over to the opposite bank. The country we were now in was highly cultivated, and we thought we should make our journey well; but the very next day as we travelled the face of the country changed by degrees, until at length a wide stretch of desert lay before us, extending to within three-fourths of a mile of the river. The heat became intense; there was no water to be had, and we began to suffer severely from thirst; so we immediately changed our road, and came down directly to the river, pursued our course again by water, and did not land until we came to the Island of Elephantina, which lies a little below the town of Assuan, and of which the soil is so good and the vegetation so rich that it is called by the natives 'Flowery Island.' Its inhabitants are an humble and courteous people; they treated us with great hospitality, and were thankful for some trifling presents which my master left with them. In that country no civility is ever received by a stranger without his making some present in return for it: the poor expect it from him as a favour, the rich demand it as a right. When we arrived at the town of Devie, a little farther up the river, the sheik to whom my master had the letter of introduction, required him to make him a present of his sword; unwilling to part with it, he offered him a watch; he took it in his hand, examined it, thanked him, but refused to keep it, saying it would be of no use to him: in which, indeed, he was right enough; for of what value could such a curious piece of work be to one who could not understand even for what purpose it was made. As it was my master's interest, both for our safety and for the furtherance of our journey, to be in good favour with him, he was obliged reluctantly to take off his own sword, (for he always wore a military dress, for the sake of protection,) and respectfully throwing the belt over the shoulder of the sheik, to beg his acceptance of it. Nothing could exceed his joy and his gratitude, and he promised to do any thing in his power to serve us; nor can I ever forget that he offered my master a present of a slave in return. My poor master, (who was humanity itself,) as you may well conceive, shrunk at the thoughts of such a thing—but in that country it is nothing unusual; though, for my part, I never could become used to seeing poor human creatures made such vile use of, just as if they were not of the same flesh and blood as ourselves. I was told, that in one part of Africa, called Dar Kulla, when the inhabitants of the neighbouring provinces go there to purchase slaves, the chief article they bring with them for that purpose is salt; and for twelve or fifteen pounds of that, they will purchase a poor innocent young creature, of about fourteen years of age, whom they will barbarously carry off from friends and family, and make undergo the severest drudgery in a strange land. Our farmers will not put as much labour on their cattle, nor give them as much ill usage, as I have seen these unfortunate creatures obliged to endure. I declare to you, if there was nothing else to make me dislike the country, this, in itself, would be enough to drive me from it for ever.

"While we remained here, a caravan was setting out from thence for the province of Darfur; it was the very thing my master wished for, so we joined it.

"On this journey we had all the suffering usual to crossing a desert country, in the hottest season of the year. One poor man, who had joined us, and was travelling on foot, came up beside my camel one evening, and asked me so pitifully for a bit of bread that if it had been my last morsel, he should have had it. 'How long have you been without bread?' said I. 'Two days,' he answered. 'And how long without water?' 'I drank water last night.' Whatever I had, I shared with him, and made him ride, by turns, on my camel, for the rest of the journey. We stopped at Cobbe, a town in Darfur: it was a market day when we arrived, and as the inhabitants of all the neighbouring towns and villages, of which there is a great number, had come into the market, the town was crowded to excess; it was just the time of the year, too, when they lay in their stock of corn; there was, consequently, a great quantity of millet for sale, and I saw two and sometimes three pecks of that grain sold for the merest trifle, frequently for even a string of beads, which would not be worth more than a penny at Cairo.

"There are four or five schools here, where the children are taught to read and write; and those of the poor are instructed free of expense.

"The inhabitants of Cobbe are mostly foreigners and merchants, who trade with Egypt; some, to be sure, are natives of the country, but, for the most part, they are settlers, come from about the borders of the Nile. During our stay here my master was robbed of a quantity of coral, by some of the people about him; he wished to be introduced to the sultan, and to lay his complaint before him. One of the chief men had assured him, that the sultan would be happy to make him amends for any loss he sustained while living in his province. This made my master the more anxious for the interview, which was unaccountably delayed, from day to day; at length he was promised admission, and desiring me to attend him, we went to the palace. We found him in a large court-yard, mounted on a white mule;—he wore a long scarlet robe, a turban of white silk, and yellow boots. His saddle was of crimson velvet, his sword very broad in the blade, and he sat holding it thrust out straight before him. He was a middle-sized man, about fifty, with very bright eyes, a thick beard, and his colour perfectly black. In a little while he retired into his palace, desiring us to follow him. My master thought now was his time, and made one of the servants lay before him a present of a piece of silk, in his name, thinking it likely the sultan would now more readily listen to him; but the other only accepted the present, saying, 'May the blessing of God be upon you,' which, I am told, is the usual answer, and then left the room; nor could my master ever afterward obtain any offer of compensation for his loss, except that once the savage sent him word that the lost property might be valued at about eight and thirty slaves. Upon my master declaring he would listen to no such terms, the sultan, after a long delay, sent him a small sum of money, five camels, and twenty oxen, altogether not of more value than one hundred and twenty piastres, while the coral which he had lost was worth seven hundred and fifty.

"After this, we quitted Darfur, with a caravan, going to Abyssinia. I need not describe this journey to you; it was like that of other caravans, slow and tiresome. After travelling many a weary day, we arrived at the borders of Abyssinia. Here we were much amused, by observing the great difference between these people and any other nation we had yet seen.

"The poorer inhabitants are quite a distinct race from the rest, and are said to be descended from the original natives of the country; they live in the open plains under a kind of shady hut, which they form for themselves, from a large tree, with very long boughs: of these long branches they will lop off those that grow long down on the stem, and then bending down the upper ones to each side, fasten the ends of them in the ground; this makes a kind of arch, one on each side of the stem, which stands up in the middle between them, and looks like a support for the whole. Under this shed they live, during the dry season of the year, for their year is divided into two parts only, the wet and the dry season.

"When the rain is going to set in, these poor people quit the open country, carry off with them their stores of provisions, and fly to the mountains, where they live in caves, until the season changes again, when they will come out, make up their little dwellings, and live there till the wet season comes around again.

"But there is one dreadful hardship these poor harmless people have to undergo, worse than any thing else that could happen to them: all the governors of the provinces, who hold offices under the king of Abyssinia, are obliged, by law, to furnish him with a certain number of slaves every year; they must get them either by force or by money, or their lives are to answer for it; and accordingly they come down yearly upon these unfortunate creatures, to carry them off. The poor people often fly to the caves in the mountains, to hide themselves; but whenever they offer the least resistance the slaughter is dreadful, for their inhuman assailants will not hesitate to put father and mother to death, and carry off the children prisoners; and this they will do till their number is complete. The age which they prefer in their captives is from twelve upward. Except to halt at the different towns, we made no stay till we reached the town of Gondar; the caravan went on, but we remained. This is a large town; I was told it is three miles long at its greatest length; the houses have all very high thatched roofs, and each has trees planted around it, which bear a profusion of fine white blossoms, so that in their flowering season the whole town appears perfectly white. My master's great object was to get to the source of the Nile; we therefore quitted Gondar, and travelled down the western side of a large lake, called Tyana. At the end of the second day we came to Mescala Christos, a large village upon the top of a hill; here we passed the night, and had a fine view of the Nile, which was not far from hence, as it flowed through the country beneath us. The governor of one of the provinces of Abyssinia was going to war with another, and was marching with his army through the country at that very time; we feared very much lest we should fall into his hands, and thought the best thing we could do was to ask his protection. This we did, and the consequence was, that he sent us a guide, on whose fidelity, he assured us, we might safely rely, and gave us every thing else that was necessary for our journey. Among other things, he sent my master a beautiful gray horse, ready bridled and saddled, ' But do not ride him,' said he, ' let him be led before you; it is the horse I rode myself yesterday; and whoever meets you will know by him that you are under my protection, and will not dare to harm you.' We set out with our guide, and travelled for some days in a southerly direction, crossed the plain called Sacula, and ascended a very steep rugged mountain; this was the worst part of our journey; it was thickly wooded, and our feet were greatly torn by thorn bushes, and a kind of bramble called the kentuffa, which is very prickly, and wounds severely. From the top of the mountain we saw the Nile winding below, but it was only like a small stream, with scarcely water enough to have turned a mill. About half a mile off was a mountain, called Geesh, at the foot of which our guide told us we should see the source. For my own part, I did long to see it, and thought it must be something wonderful, and my master was all impatience. As we descended into the plain, which lay before us, and through which the river ran, he called out to the guide, ' As you value your life, show me where the spring is from which the Nile flows.' The guide, astonished at his earnestness, pointed out a small green hillock, which lay a little beyond us; ' In that,' said he, ' are the two fountains of the Nile; but if you approach them, take off your shoes, for such is the custom of the people.' My master said nothing, but, throwing off his shoes, darted off like lightning from me. I flung off mine too, and followed as fast as I could fly. We stopped at the fountain, stooped down, and each took a draught of the water. ' Jackson,' said he, ' it will be something for you to tell, when you return home, that you have drunk of the fountain of the Nile.' The very name of home, and I in this distant land, filled my mind with tender emotions, and I felt the tears start into my eyes. I believe my master saw it, for he said, very kindly, to me, ' Come,

Jackson, come, I hope we shall both see our native land yet.' A little while after we turned away from the fountain, and proceeded to the town of Geesh, which was not more than six hundred yards from us; here we stopped for the night, and were most hospitably recei ed by the chief of the town. I had almost forgotten to tell you that the religion of the Abyssinians is a corrupt mixture of Christianity with Mohammedan and pagan superstitions; and though Christianity was early planted in their country, yet the debasing influence of the neighbouring Mohammedan and pagan nations has left little among them but its name.

" My master's curiosity was now satisfied; he had seen the source of the Nile, and he had drunk of the water; a pleasure, he told me, which had been enjoyed by few Europeans before us. I own I did not feel so much as he, but there is something in doing what few have done before you, which makes a man think better of himself. I had seen the Nile at its greatest breadth; I could now step over it; and though I don't think the sight was worth all the trouble and danger we went through, still I remember, with satisfaction, that I am one of the few who have visited that interesting spot. I thought my master had got enough of travelling, and that he would now be content to take the shortest course back to Cairo, whence we should sail homeward, but he entertained far different views. At one time he was for crossing Africa, from east to west, arriving at Tombuctoo, and following the river Niger to the sea coast; and he thought, as I had been there before, I could be of great assistance to him. However, this plan was attended with so many dangers, and he could gain so little information from the savage people around him, that, to my great joy, he gave it up. I recollect he put the question to one of the chiefs, and got the following answer: 'The journey you propose is full of danger: don't think more of it; I will answer for you for four days' journey eastward from Darfur; but after that all is wilderness, and no man knows if he be to meet a friend or a foe.' You will not think it at all wonderful that I had no desire to pay a second visit to a place where I had suffered so much. His next resolution was more agreeable; it was to take a course due east, which he hoped would bring us to the Straits of Babelmandel, by which the Red Sea is joined to the Indian Ocean, and we therefore busily set about getting all the information the people could give us, and making the necessary preparation for our departure. Once arrived at the straits, we were to be guided by circumstances; his wish was to meet a ship which would be sailing south, along the eastern coast of Africa, and thus to reach the Cape of Good Hope, which is the most southern part of the African continent. At the worst, he was tolerably sure of getting a passage in one of the vessels which go up the Red Sea, and carry the merchandise of India to the Isthmus of Suez. Accordingly, in a few days we set out, attended by a strong party of slaves, who were now returning from Gondar. Nothing remarkable occurred for the first three days, but on the fourth we were passing through a country full of wild beasts. My master and I joined a party who were going to hunt the elephant. Every one was mounted on horseback. We were about thirty in number, and set out an hour before daybreak. Some of the men, who were elephant hunters by profession, rode double, that is to say, two on each horse. These are light, active fellows: and as soon as we came up with an elephant, they advanced, to close in upon him. Two of them then (who are mounted on the one horse) will get before him, and prevent him from making his escape, by facing him, and crossing his path from side to side, whichever way he turns. The poor animal, exasperated by the interruption, tries to revenge himself on the horse, but this the rider dexterously avoids; at length the man who is riding hindmost slips down off the horse, and, getting behind the elephant, with his sword cuts the back sinews of his heel across; this completely disables him; he is unable to advance a step; the hunters all press forward on him, and quickly put him to death with their javelins. After he is killed, his flesh is cut into long thin pieces, about the thickness of a man's finger, and the natives hang it up, dry it, and use it for food during the wet season. I have seen it hanging on the boughs of trees, beside the shady huts I have described them living in, and for a long time could not think what it was they always had there, nor what use such a hard tough substance could be—and hard enough it is—for, though in cooking it they pound and beat it with a wooden mallet, then boil, and afterward lay it on the fire to roast, as we do potatoes, yet, after all, it is little better than a stick.

"After these delays, we proceeded directly forward, nor stopped till we reached the sea. We were many days longer on our journey than we expected, having been advised, instead of going to the Straits, to make for a town called Berbera, upon the coast, where a large fair is held every year, and is attended by caravans, who come from a great distance inland. One of them we met on our journey; and as my master's visit to the springs of the Nile had made his name known to some of the principal men of the caravan, they readily gave us protection. Berbera is the principal town of the Somanli, who are a very active and industrious race; my master told me they trafficked with foreign countries, selling gum, myrrh, and other things of that kind, and he was, therefore, not without hope of finding a vessel that would take us aboard,—nor was he disappointed. We found a French merchantman there, which was going to sail in a few days for Fort Dauphiny, in the southern part of Madagascar, a very large island which is separated from the east coast of Africa by the channel of Mosambique. The captain said he intended to touch at two places on the coast of Africa, and hoped my master would not object to the delay; but he little knew my master's plan, for it was the very thing to give him pleasure. Having set sail, it now appeared as if every thing was to favour us; the wind was fair, the weather moderate, and in due time we reached Quiloa. This had been once the chief town in this part of Africa (which is called Zanguebar) for from it the Portuguese used to get their slaves; and the merchants, who used to deal in human flesh, lived there. We heard that ten thousand was formerly the number annually exported, it has now sunk to a few hundreds. From Quiloa we went to Mosambique, which lies also on the coast, but considerably to the south. This is a settlement belonging to Portugal, which trades with the natives for gold and elephants' teeth."

"That must be a fine country where gold is to be bought; of course it is very cheap?" said old Jackson. "As cheap, sir, as you could desire it. About one hundred years ago, the natives on receiving toys and glass beads, dug a hole in the ground, into which they put these articles: then, taking them out, they filled the same hole with gold dust, and gave it in exchange. Elephants' teeth, which give the ivory, was bartered for the same bulk in cloth; but the price of these things was much higher when I was there; however, you should not be too ready to think a country happy because gold is cheap. If gold in Mosambique was as plenty as coals with us, I should think it dear. The gold might be exchanged for a very small sum of money, but you would also have to pay your life into the bargain. Would you believe that robbers, whom the Portuguese sentence to death, are often, as a milder punishment, transported to Mosambique, where five or six years is thought a long life. I saw a fort there, with a great many pieces of cannon, but they were quite unfit for service. In the house where the governor lived my master dined, and there was a great appearance of riches. Tea was served in cups and saucers of pure gold, and the negro attendants wore a great many ornaments of the same metal.

I saw at Mosambique some natives of Mapooa, a very large district inland. They are a very strong made people, and have a fine look. They adorn their skin by tattooing it, that is, marking it with great scars, and the welts they thus make often rise considerably above the skin. They file their teeth to a point, so as to give the whole set the appearance of a coarse saw. They wear their hair in very strange shapes—sometimes showing one side, sometimes both sides, with a crest stretching across from the brow to the neck; sometimes leaving only a tuft on the top. More inland than these, (indeed, I was told it was a journey of forty days to arrive there,) lived the Monjou;—these are negroes of a deep shining black, with high cheek-bones, and small tufts of woolly hair on their heads. This was all the information we were able to gain by a stay of a fortnight at Mosambique; I was, therefore, glad enough when the captain told us the vessel was ready to sail. He had taken in a quantity of gold dust and ivory, which the natives exchange for salt, shells, tobacco, and beaver cloth; so we weighed anchor, and set the helm for sailing around the south of Madagascar, to Port Dauphiny. For some days we proceeded as favourably as we could wish, and nothing remarkable happened until we had reached the latitude which was necessary for doubling the island. It then, however, began to blow a gale, which for five days continued to increase. I had been in a storm before, but it was nothing compared to the violence of this. At one time the ship was raised on a mountain of water, and the next instant plunged into a depth from which she was raised again to the clouds by the next wave. We had several mishaps; a sudden shift of the wind tore away our rudder, carried away the main yard, and obliged us to drive before the wind on bare poles, for some time, but there was no actual danger. Our ship was sound, the captain a skilful seaman, and we had plenty of sea room: however, one evil attended it, we were driven out of our course. Nor, though we soon repaired the helm, could we for a moment think of putting about, till we had reached the latitude of 30° south, and 35° east longitude. This was opposite the coast of Caffraria, not very far from the Cape of Good Hope,—that is, though it was many days' journey to the Cape, my master had hopes, if set ashore, of reaching it in safety.

He therefore said to the captain, 'If you go direct to Port Bourbon, I must take my passage from that to the Cape of Good Hope, and perhaps may be obliged to wait some time before an opportunity offers. We are now, according to your reckoning, little more than one hundred and fifty miles from the coast of Caffraria: draw near the land, and set me and my servant ashore, and I will make it worth your while.' When two honest men come together they are seldom long in striking a bargain :—one says what he expects to receive, the other what he thinks it right to give ; and as both are men of conscience, they have no huckstering. Behold us then seated in the long boat, quitting the ship with all our baggage, and about to land in a part of Africa where but few Europeans have ever been. As we approached the land, we could see a number of natives who had collected together at the sight of a boat. They were armed with spears, and accompanied by dogs, but when my master stood up in the boat and waved a white handkerchief, they at once laid aside their arms, and made signs to show us where we might land in safety. They then surrounded us with great appearance of curiosity, desirous of knowing our intentions, but with great kindness. We should have found it difficult to let them know our wishes, if there had not been in the boat's crew a Dutchman who understood French, and among the Caffres a Hottentot who spoke Dutch. In this way, therefore, my master's wishes were made known to them, and they agreed, for a stated reward to be paid them at the Cape, to conduct us there in safety. Every thing being thus settled, the boat returned to the vessel, the men having received some valuable marks of my master's good will. Indeed I should mention to you, that my master always took care to have the means of rewarding those whom he found it necessary to ask for assistance, supplying himself with trinkets of various kinds, which were easily carried by him, and could also be easily turned into money by those to whom he gave them. It was the month of June, which is the depth of winter in that country, the natives therefore soon kindled a fire of dried bushes, by whirling briskly a pointed stick against another piece laid flat on the ground, and having a hole in it, to receive the pointed stick, they then presented us with a bullock, which we were obliged to roast whole, our hosts stopping to take share of their own gift. On the next morning we set out with two guides and a party, who were to conduct us to the nearest settlement of Europeans. Our road lay through a country wooded on all sides, as far as the eye could reach. The cattle also appeared in such numbers as to defy calculation, and they were equal in condition to the best-fed oxen I have ever seen in our Dublin markets. We saw no sheep, nor could we observe any marks of farming work going on. The surrounding country was of great extent, bounded by mountains. Our guides explained to us, that we

Africa. p. 132

Residence of a horde of Caffres.

could, on no account, travel early, as the wild beasts, with which the country abounds, rise with the sun, and then range the desert in quest of prey. In our course we struck inland, for the purpose of getting fresh water, that on the coast being generally brackish. Having gone about thirty-five miles the second day, we wished to rest for the night, for my master was very much tired. Our guides told us that the place was the haunt of leopards, and if they scented us out, nothing could prevent them from destroying some of us. We made our fire larger, therefore, and began to consult on the best way of guarding against danger, when sleep overcame us, and we remained quiet till the next morning, notwithstanding the danger with which we were threatened. No sooner, however, was the sun risen than we saw how well grounded was the precaution of our guides. On every side we saw the tracks of lions, tigers, and elephants, and had not the goodness of Providence saved us, we should inevitably have been torn to pieces.

"At noon of that day we came up with a horde of Caffres, that were said by our guides to belong to a bad tribe, and presently after we were stopped by twelve of them, armed with spears, and clothed in leopard skins: one of them came up to me and attempted to snatch a knife, which I had slung over my shoulder; this, however, I stoutly resisted, which threw him into such a rage that he raised his lance apparently to kill me. He wore a leopard's skin, his black face was daubed with red ochre, his eyes seemed starting from their sockets, and he gnashed his teeth. In short, if I was inclined to be passionate, I think his appearance would have completely cured me. That must be very sinful, thought I, which can make a man so unlike any thing human: fortunately, another chief came up, who turned aside the point of his weapon, and making signs to me to give him the knife, he told us to cross the river, which lay before us, as quietly as possible. This was the boundary of the Caffres' country, and south of it we were safe from these people. In this way we still kept advancing by day, at night making a barricade against the wild animals, and lighting all around us prodigious fires. Our sleep, however, was disturbed by a herd of elephants brushing through a neighbouring wood, and trampling with their monstrous feet on every thing that stood in their way; but this was not our only cause for terror; we had to pass through a part of the Bushmen's territory, who live by plunder, and attack, with poisoned arrows, such as come in their way: these are a very small race of men, not more than four feet and a half high, but uncommonly strong and active. The Caffres, whom we had just left, are seldom less than five feet eight inches high, and are remarkably well made: their colour is nearly black, and they have neither the thick lip, nor the woolly hair of the Negro, but the Bushmens are low, ill made, and have very ugly countenances. Their clothing is merely the raw skin of a sheep or a goat, which is fastened on by a belt. They wear around their ancles thongs of raw skin, but their hair is unlike that of any other human beings, not covering the whole head, but growing in little separate tufts here and there."

" Did your master ever ask your guides what was the cause of this difference?"

" He did, but the answer did not seem to satisfy him. The guides said that it was always so,—that their parents had been so before them; but my master thought it more likely that hunger and cold had so stunted their growth,—for having no disposition to settle down to a quiet life and till the ground for their food, but choosing rather to live by plunder, they are driven from the more fertile parts of the valley, and obliged to take shelter in the high lands, where food is very scarce. They sometimes collect in parties of thirty or forty, said our guides, and attack the farmers' cattle. On these occasions they carry a small bow and quiver full of poisoned arrows, which, when they are actually fighting, they stick in a band of sheep-skin around the head. If they are successful in carrying off any cattle, they quickly cut them up, and make a feast, which collects all the carrion crows, kites, and vultures, within a great distance; indeed, it is by this that the farmer knows the road he is to take in pursuit. When they fail in their plundering expeditions, they pursue the larger kinds of game, some drive them into narrow passes, where others are waiting to strike them with their poisoned arrows. Sometimes they dig pit-falls, which they cover over with earth or grass; and when all their endeavours fail, they are obliged to feed on ants' eggs, caterpillars, and locusts, with various kinds of bitter roots. It is not wonderful, therefore, that with such fare their bodies should be insufficiently nourished and dwarfish, nor will you be surprised, that through the country which they infest we were obliged to travel with circumspection. Fortunately we met none of them, though every now and then our guides pointed out spots where they had committed some atrocity. In this manner we proceeded for some days without observing any thing extraordinary, when at length one of the guides suddenly shouted, 'I see a Hottentot guarding sheep.' We all immediately hastened to the spot where he was, and observed him tending a flock of at least four thousand, and in a short time our joy was increased by finding ourselves in the farm house of a European. He was a Dutchman, and certainly did not want the inclination, any more than the means, of being hospitable.

"He was owner of five thousand acres, for which he paid no more rent than a farthing an acre: yet I should be sorry, if I had but one acre at home, to live in so dirty and uncomfortable a manner as he did. His house contained two rooms, one was kitchen and parlour, and the other the sleeping room; and they were separated by a matted partition. In the first we found two fresh-killed sheep, hanging near the fire place, while the pool of blood be neath them, and every thing about showed us they were not very nice in their way of living. The floor was of clay, in the hollows of which were splashes of sour milk and mud, and there were two holes in the wall for windows, but without any glass. In one corner was sitting a hen, in another a duck and her young ones, and in a third were half a dozen dogs, who every now and then began to bark loudly, running out into the farm yard, which was ancle deep in mud, and returning wet and dirty, and sprinkling us all over. Outside the house, at some little distance, were several straw huts, where the servants lived, and between both, the spacious pen in which his cattle were shut up at night, to defend them from the wild beasts. The dung of these pens must have been collecting for years, for it rose to the very roof of the house, and, perhaps by this time, rises far above it, for he never would think of cleaning it away." " O Tom, what a nice garden he might have about his house with such manure; what fine fields of wheat and potatoes." " That he never dreams of; his cattle find plenty of grazing without his taking any trouble, and as for vegetables, he never uses them. He lives upon meat at breakfast, dinner, and supper; and, as my master said, this sufficiently accounts for his indolence, such food always making a man dull and inactive." " And how far does he live from any town where he can supply himself with what he wants?" " Why, between five and six hundred miles, and he is not less than a long day's journey from any neighbour." "Well, Tom, we may excuse him for not having a garden where he has such plenty of food, which, perhaps, he likes better; but I can find no apology for such slovenly habits, and for his total neglect of every decency and comfort." "Away at such a distance from society, it might be too much to expect that his furniture should be very nice; but cleanliness, when there is water at hand, is always within our reach; indeed, I wonder he would not himself feel it much more comfortable, as I am sure it is more healthful to be clean than dirty. And yet, though the distance is so great, he often sets out for the Cape with his large wagon, drawn by oxen, and filled with butter, soap, (which he manufactures himself from the fat of the animals he kills,) ostrich feathers, the skins of wild beasts, and the potash which he provides by burning vegetables, which he exchanges for a little coffee, brandy, and gunpowder." "Well, Tom, as he brings soap to such a distant market, it is to be supposed he uses a little of it on himself?" "Not a bit, judging from his appearance: he has the heavy look of indolence—his person is bulky and unwieldy, and all his motions slow. His dress is a loose unbuttoned jacket, like a sailor's, which he hangs over his shoulders; it would be hard to say of what colour is his shirt, and as he wears his collar always open, you see his sun-burned neck and breast; his breeches are made of undressed skin, as well as his shoes; stockings he never uses, and, to crown all, has an enormous hat, with his tobacco pipe stuck in the band of it, except when in his mouth, which is more frequently the case."

"And what sort of people are the Hottentots, Tom? You know we have it as a nickname for any one who is very uncivil in his manners."

"We cannot expect them to be like us, father, since they have not had our advantages, but as a nickname, it might as well be given to every uncivilized people. They were formerly the original owners of the country, and were very numerous; but having either been driven out by the Dutch, when they took possession of the country, or reduced to slavery, there are not now more than twenty thousand in the whole colony. Nothing could equal the cruelty with which the planters used to treat them; a severe whipping was the punishment for the slightest fault, and the flogging was not determined by the number of lashes, but by the pipes their masters smoked during the operation. Poor creatures, my master told me they used to be worked hard, had bad fare, were treated more like beasts than men, until a short time before we were there, when the British, getting possession of the Cape, did away slavery, and encouraged them to come and settle near the Cape. They are found to be mild, honest, and faithful. They are, indeed, very timid, but my master said that was caused by the cruelty of their former masters. They were generally thought to be a stupid race, but lately the governor formed a number of them into a regiment, and they proved not only as well behaved as the British soldiers, but as cleanly: their clothes, arms, and their persons being as neat and in as good order as any I ever saw." "And yet, Tom, I recollect myself to have heard that they were a filthy people, daubing their bodies all over with grease." "You heard what was very true—their habits were very dirty, but my master said we should remember they had never been taught better; they used to cut their meat into strips, a yard or two long, and slightly warming them over the fire, they ate them as we would a radish. The grease they rub over their bodies to protect them from the sun and from insects, but the readiness they now show to get rid of their sheep-skin clothes, and to keep their persons clean, shows that it was only the neglect and severity of the European settlers, and the want of water, which made them so dirty. When young, they are by no means ill-looking; but as they grow old, both men and women, the latter especially, lose their shape, and become remarkably fat. It is true, they are so very indolent that even hunger sometimes will not rouse them, and yet so kind and affectionate at the same time are they as to share their last morsel with a companion.— But to return to my story, from which I have wandered so far. The trees around the farmer's house were hung with the skins of almost every kind of wild animals; lions, tigers, panthers, and elephants, which he had killed in the neighbourhood: for a farmer never stirs abroad without an enormous musket; and so expert a marksman is he that he seldom fails to bring down his object with a single ball. The old man bore many a mark of the dangers he was exposed to, and entertained us very much by the account of his escapes. When about forty years of age, he shot a lion in a narrow pass of a wood, which immediately fell without his observing that there were two together. The other lion rushed instantly upon him before he had time to reload his piece, and not only wounded him with his sharp claws, but tore him in such a dreadful manner that he lay senseless. The lion, it is said, does not mangle a body which it supposes dead, except when obliged by hunger; it therefore left him, and he was shortly after carried home by his servants. When we saw him he was in perfect health, but he never recovered the use of his arm. He still, however, could fire his musket, and told us that in travelling from the Cape he has often killed four or five elephants. 'I always aim,' said he, 'at the breast, and generally kill the animal in one shot; but should I hit it in either of the fore legs, so as to break it, I must fire again.'

" He told us another story of himself, which was well worth hearing. It will show how cool and steady these men become by long practice with the gun, and being used to meet with wild beasts. It was about a couple of years before he met with the accident that lamed him, that his wife was sitting within the house, near the door, the children playing about her, and he himself outside, mending one of his wagons, when, suddenly, though it was about twelve o'clock in the day, a very large lion came up, and laid himself down quietly in the shade, upon the very threshhold of the door. His wife, frightened almost to death, and knowing the danger of making any attempt to fly, remained in her chair, without moving, and the children hid themselves in her lap. Their cry drew the farmer's attention, and he ran toward the door; but think how great must have been his astonishment when he found the lion lying right across it Although the animal had not seen him, it seemed impossible to escape, unarmed as he was. He had thought enough, however, to creep gently to the side of the house, to the window of his room, where, fortunately, he had set his loaded gun that morning; but the opening was too small for him to get in by; the door of the room, however, was open, so that he could see the lion's motions. At that moment it was beginning to stir, perhaps with the design of making a spring upon his wife and children. There was no time to be lost; so he said softly to the mother not to be alarmed, and calling upon the Almighty, fired his piece. The ball passed directly over the hair of the eldest boy's head, and lodged in the forehead of the lion immediately above his eyes, stretching him on the ground, so that he never stirred more.

The next morning our kind host provided my

master with a wagon, two sets of oxen, eight in each set, a couple of Hottentot drivers, together with provisions enough to serve us the better part of our journey. On our road, many places were pointed out to us as the particular haunt of wild beasts; but though dreadful to a European, they are less formidable than a Bushman to a Hottentot. At our next resting place, I had an opportunity of seeing one of these Bushmen, who had been taken prisoner, when an infant, by one of the colony, and brought up at his house. He was now twenty-five years old, and not more that four feet two inches high. His make was strong and clumsy, but no greyhound could be swifter in running When the number of Bushmen is strong enough they attack the Hottentots and Caffrarians whenever they meet them. They use a bow and arrows; the latter dipped in such a mortal poison that I was told nothing could cure the wound.

"In about sixteen days after we found ourselves among our countrymen. You know how long I had been a stranger to them, and may well believe with what joy I saw the soldiers mounting guard before the governor's house, and heard my own language spoken by almost every one about me. Need I say that I did not forget to return thanks to that almighty Being who had preserved me from so many secret and open dangers, and had given me strength to bear up under such cruel sufferings, and brought me safe out of a land of bondage I thought of you, father, and of my mother; and, though I was still many thousand miles from you, I felt as if my arrival among my countrymen had brought me many a day's journey nearer to home.

"Capetown is built on the side of two hills: one is called the Table Mountain, and the other the Lion Mountain. We were glad to get into a town with wide streets again; but the thatched roofs gave the houses the oddest appearance; and these are not made with straw, like ours, but with reeds and rushes. I was told they cannot use tiled or slated roofs, on account of the hurricanes; as, when they are blown off by a storm, they do a great deal of damage in falling. The town contains about one thousand one hundred houses, which are built with great regularity. The chief want the inhabitants suffer, is a scarcity of wood, either for building or for firing. Indeed, for the latter purpose, the more wealthy families keep a slave, whose sole business it is to gather fagots on the neighbouring mountains. Their tables are well supplied with butchers' meat, fresh game, and fruit. My master was anxious to make some short journeys up the country, and hired strong covered wagons, which is the usual mode of conveyance here for travellers. They were furnished with every thing necessary for our accommodation on the road; mattresses, vessels for cooking our food, gunpowder, tea, coffee, and a great quantity of such things as might be required for making presents to the natives, such as beads, toys, trinkets, &c. These great wagons were drawn by ten oxen each, and were driven by Hottentots. Before I describe our journey, I should tell you something of the nature of the country. Behind Capetown rises a chain of mountains; beyond that is another, with a valley lying between the two; and farther on still, is another range of mountains, and again another valley lies between. These valleys are called karroos; and, after the rainy season, become uncommonly beautiful. The vegetation at that time is so rich, that they are filled with the sweetest flowers, especially in the great Karroo, which is the valley that lies at the foot of the farthest chain of mountains. We took our road first in an easterly direction, so as to wind around the mountains. It was a matter of the greatest amusement and curiosity to us to watch the different kinds of strange-looking animals that we met with on this journey. There were numerous troops of bubales, antelopes, and zebras, and a vast number of ostriches. I am sure, all together, we did not see less than between four and five thousand, including the different species of each. There is a kind of antelope there which much resembles our goat, but that it is of a pale blue colour; they are very rare, and we thought ourselves fortunate to see one on the second day of our journey. We passed a mountain called the Pearl Berg, which takes its name from a chain of large white stones, looking, at a distance, like a string of pearls, which goes up the side of the mountain, and passes over its summit. One of these stones is called by way of distinction, *the* pearl, on account of its size, being four hundred feet high, and full a mile around. In the clefts of this rock a great profusion of plants, of different kinds, are growing. The whole mountain is thickly covered with vegetation, and large flights of a beautiful bird called the creeper may be seen hovering over it, come to suck the honey from the sugar-maple tree.

" Near the mountain rivers we often saw great numbers of the white pelican, as well as of the rose-coloured flamingo, whose wings are used as fans for flapping away the flies, which in this country swarm dreadfully. Turning around a ledge of rocks one day, we encountered a troop of not less than four or five hundred large black baboons, lying basking in the sun. The frightful creatures started up instantly, giving the most dreadful howls, and clambered up the rocks, as fast as possible. We had now arrived at the entrance of the great Karroo—such a dreary stretch of barren land as lay before us I never in my life saw, except in the African deserts. Not a habitation was to be seen; the ground was parched and burst into a thousand cracks by the heat of the sun. There was nothing growing there of any kind, and we found the soil covered with thick brown dust, which, upon inquiry, my master told me was actually the ashes of withered plants of last year, which had been dried and burned by the sun, until they were reduced to powder. It was well for us that our wagons were made on purpose to serve us for houses to live in, for there was not another shelter of any kind to be had; and the very first night we were there the wet season set in. My master had no idea it was so near at hand. Such rain as fell, you can have no idea of. Fortunately we had provisions enough with us; for, I am sure, this barren place could not have afforded us a mouthful. And now, during the rain, we could not put our heads outside the wagon roofs; we found tolerable shelter, however, under the rocks for the cattle; and, as to our Hottentot drivers, they ran up the mountains, and hid in caves, until the rains should cease; my master giving to each a portion of food, to carry away with him, and they in return promising faithfully to come back to him; which indeed they did to a man.

"In a few days the rain became, by degrees, less and less violent; soon it ceased, and it was really curious to see the rapid progress of vegetation, appearing over the same ground that a short time before was so dry and barren. In a little while the whole place appeared green and fresh: day after day the plants sprang up thicker and thicker: their buds burst, their leaves spread, and their blossoms began to appear; the warmth of the sun soon brought them into full bloom, and in a day or two more the whole place was like one great garden. The air was so sweet, and the thousands and thousands of flowers, of every colour in the rainbow, that were there, I thought the most beautiful sight

I ever witnessed in my life. By this time, down came all the poor herdsmen, who live upon the mountains, glad to feed their cattle upon these fresh young herbs; and it was amusing, also, to see the troops of tall ostriches come stalking in to look for their share of the feast; the antelopes, likewise, came bounding down the mountains to feed; and so busy, and, indeed, so beautiful a scene I could not have conceived,—the animals all looked so happy—the flowers and herbs so fresh. The only thing we had to regret was, that in one short month it would be all over; for the sun is here so powerful that even in that space of time the flowers begin to fade again. However, I should tell you how the wisdom and goodness of God have provided a still farther supply for these poor parched animals, who have been living upon dry mountain food for eleven months of the year. Even after the green herbs begin to fail them in the Karroo, there still remain several kinds of very juicy plants, which do not fade so soon as the others; and, among them, one shrub, which gives a kind of milky juice, that quenches their thirst, and is, besides, very nourishing. I am told that each of these shrubs affords not less than a pint of liquor.

"You may well suppose my master had no mind to stay and see this delightful scene fade away. Just as it was beginging to change, we quitted it for ever, and took our road back again to Capetown. Nothing remarkable occurred until we were about half way on our journey, when I observed to my master that the drivers were not now returning by the same way they had come. 'I have given them orders to that effect,' said he; 'I wish to visit a village which lies in this direction, and which is, indeed, worth every one's going to see. I inquired why, and he told me the spot where it stands was formerly a perfect wilderness; and that he would now find there a thriving village, containing two hundred and fifty-six cottages and tents, and near one thousand three hundred Hottentot inhabitants; all cleanly, active, industrious, and pious. 'I told you before,' said he, 'that these poor ignorant people were well disposed, and easily led aright, if they had but instruction; and now I will show you the truth of this:—A few years ago, some pious good men quitted England for this country, determined to try what they could do among the Hottentots. They settled themselves here, and collected a few of these people about them. By degrees they induced them to build houses, and to give up the wild kind of life to which they had been accustomed; soon the good example began to spread, some more joined them, and, in a while longer, they were seen flocking into the town. The number of houses increased with the inhabitants. These good men next began to teach them different trades; tried to make them know the comforts and the blessings of honest industry; and, above all, did not fail to give them every instruction in religion. Such (said he) is the account I have heard of this village, but we shall presently see it ourselves.' We soon after entered it, and it was delightful to see a people living so comfortably and so peaceably together;—every cottage has its garden, and it is a sure sign of the industry of its owner when this looks clean and in good order. A few of the poorer class still clothe themselves in sheep skins; but those who have learned a trade, and who are industrious, pride themselves on having jackets and trowsers, and other articles of European dress, which they always wear on Sundays. The women had woollen petticoats, cotton jackets with long sleeves, and either wear caps, or a head dress made with handkerchiefs neatly folded around and around their heads; and if you go into their cottages at meal times, you will always find them say grace, both before and after eating. There is a church at the head of every street, and their clergy all live together in one large house in the town, and set a good example of industry to the people, by working in their own garden; ay, and by going every day to oversee the labour done in the different manufactories. The principal trades that I saw carried on there were those in iron work; especially the manufacture of knives, at which the Hottentots had become very expert. The people have also been taught something of agriculture; and there are water-mills in the town, to which all the corn is brought for grinding, and I was told that the quantity that passes through these mills every year was more than enough for the support of the whole town. The people are, as you may suppose, greatly attached to their good protectors and instructers. While we were there, one of these gentlemen left it for England; and nothing could equal the grief of the people at parting from him—numbers of them pressed forward, offering him some little gift as a keep-sake, and entreating him to return again to them: the children of the different schools cried bitterly, and when at last he stepped into the wagon, the inhabitants of the town crowded around it, and as he slowly drove away, upward of two hundred voices sang at once a farewell hymn to him.*

"We quitted this place next morning, and continued our road, without interruption, till we got back again to Capetown."

"Well, Tom, your master was, I suppose, willing now to return to Europe. After seeing so much, he was glad, I suspect, to return to the comforts of home. A good bed, a clean table cloth, and a decent meal, are not, perhaps, enough valued by those who know not what it is to want them; but that was neither his case nor yours."

"I confess honestly, father, I began to cast

* The various missionary societies are doing much good in this country. In 1831 the Moravians had six missionary stations, thirty-six missionaries, and nearly three thousand converts. The London Missionary Society had then twenty missionaries, and six hundred and twenty-one native communicants. The Wesleyan Missionary Society had fifteen missionaries besides assistants.—Am. Ed.

a longing look toward home. I had traversed the deep, climbed mountains, crossed rivers, and seen the source of the Nile. I had seen quite enough to satisfy me; but it was not so with my master; as long as the Almighty gave him health and strength, he was resolved to visit those parts of Africa which he had not as yet seen; and when he asked me if I would be content to leave him, I could not answer yes. 'There is a vessel,' said he, 'in the bay, which sails in a week for the Gambia River, between five and six hundred miles from the place where the Caledonia was wrecked. It is the place from which the greater part of those negroes who are slaves in the sugar islands in the West Indies have been brought. And I have, also, another reason, that is, to discover the source of the great river Niger; which, although many have succeeded in tracing for a great way, they have never been able to follow to its termination. Some think it runs into the great desert, and is lost in the sand; others, that the Zaire is the river by which it discharges itself into the sea. And again there are a great many very wise men who think it joins one of the arms of the river Nile. Which of these opinions is the just one, I am unable to say; but I am resolved, if possible, to find it out; and I have engaged a passage in her for us both. She goes afterward to England, so that, if you wish, you may continue your voyage homeward, but I have great hopes you will not refuse to stay with me. That part of Africa once explored, my own intention is to return to England, and you may depend on my making an addition to your wages, which I am glad you have never drawn from me. It will make a handsome some of money when you go back to your father's cottage.' The end of it was, I promised not to leave him; so immediately I began to prepare for our departure.

"On the day appointed, we set sail, and, after as favourable a voyage as could be desired, though you must not suppose the distance short, for it was above three thousand miles, we anchored at Jillifree, a town on the north bank of the Gambia, and two days after sailed up the river to Vintain, where we found a great trade carrying on with the natives for bees' wax, which is collected in the woods by the Feloops, a wild race of people. In the river we saw alligators, and also the hippopotamus, which, though not so tall as the elephant, is much longer, and more bulky. At Pisania, higher up the river, my master stopped a few days with some English merchants who resided there, with their black servants; from them he collected the necessary information for his journey; and, finding that he had arrived at the proper time for undertaking it, the rainy season being just now over, we set forward, my master and I being provided with horses, while our guides were mounted on asses. Our baggage consisted of provisions for a few days, some amber and tobacco, a compass, a couple of fowling pieces, two pair of pistols, and a few articles of clothing."

"Now that you have brought me among new acquaintances, Tom, you must tell me how they dress; of course they don't go naked?"

"The dress of both men and women is made of cotton cloth, of their own manufacture. That of the men is a loose frock, with drawers, which come half way down the leg; they wear sandals on their feet, and white cotton caps on their heads. The women's dress is a petticoat, which comes down to the ancles, and a cloak, which they wear over the bosom and shoulders. Near the Gambia, the head dress is a bandage of cotton cloth, wrapped many times over the forehead; the head is adorned with strings of white beads, with a small plate of gold in the middle of the forehead. At Medina we halted some days, and found the people not only simple but affectionate. My master waited on the king, who received him with great kindness. He was seated on a mat in front of his hut; his attendants, ranged on each side, were singing and clapping their hands. My master required permission to pass through his country, which the king not only granted at once, but told him he would offer up prayers for his safety. On this, one of the attendants began an Arabic song, and at the end of each verse the king himself, and all the people present, struck their hands against their foreheads, and said with devout and affecting solemnity, Amen."

"But, Tom, what kind of towns are those

that you were now visiting?—not, of course, like the Hottentot villages; nor, on the other hand, friendly as the towns of Barbary."

"Like all other African towns in this part of the world, Medina is surrounded by a high wall of clay; the houses are mere hovels; a circular wall of mud, four feet high, above which is a roof of bamboo cane, thatched, which rises like a sugar loaf. Their furniture is equally simple, a bundle of canes, resting upon feet, covered with a mat, or a bullock's hide, serves them for their bed; a water jar, some earthen pots, wooden bowls, and a couple of low stools, complete their stock of necessaries."

"Did you find the water scarce in this part of Africa?"

"No: there are here some large rivers which supply that necessary of-life in abundance; but when we left the course of these streams we were obliged to have negroes to carry water. After leaving Medina nothing material occurred till we reached Tallakee, the frontier town of Bondou, the inhabitants of which get a comfortable subsistence by furnishing provisions to the caravans that pass, and by the sale of ivory. Here my master was invited to a wrestling match, which was given in honour of his arrival; for they considered the appearance of a white man among them as calling for these public ceremonies. The spectators ranged themselves in a circle around the wrestlers, who were strong and active young men: they had no dress on but a pair of drawers, and their bodies had been made supple with oil, so that I think few white men could have thrown him who conquered. To this diversion succeeded a dance, in which all the performers had small bells fastened to their arms and legs, and as they kept very good time to the drum, I assure you, it made a pleasing music.

"It was in this part of our course that we saw a great many crocodiles, some of which were five and twenty feet in length. These animals were peculiarly fierce, and yet the natives are not afraid to attack them, even in their own element, as we had an opportunity of observing. A crocodile had for some days infested a particular part of the river, and seized several of the cattle belonging to the inhabitants of the village, as they drank at midday, the time when they are always watered. To rid himself and his neighbours of this enemy, a negro, having rolled a thick ox-hide around his left arm, and taken a two-edged knife, or dagger, in his right, fearlessly entered the water, and was immediately assailed by the crocodile, who raised his head a couple of feet out of the water, and opened his monstrous jaws for the purpose of seizing him. This was the moment the negro expected; he instantly thrust his left arm down the animal's throat, and the thick folds of the hide preventing his biting, he stabbed it repeatedly in the belly, where the skin is less hard than on the back, and soon dragged it lifeless to the bank.

"Provisions are very cheap in this part of the

country. I saw a bullock bought for six small lumps of amber. The next day we went to a village on the banks of the Faleme. The principal mode of livelihood there is by fishing, and they catch all the fish in long baskets, made of slight cane, placed where the current of the stream is strongest. The force of the water carries down the fish, and they are caught in these baskets, which are generally near twenty feet long, and when once the fish are in, they cannot get out. As for the smaller kinds, they are taken in great numbers in hand-nets, which are made of cotton. They generally prepare their fish for use, by pounding it in a mortar; then, having left it to dry in the sun, they make it up in large pieces, as large as our loaf bread, and when it is to be used they cut off a bit, dissolve it in boiling water, and mix it up with some other drink; but they don't eat it plain by itself.

"We went next to Fatteconda, the principal town of the province of Bondou, where the king received my master, seated under a large shady tree. He was very courteous, and showed the greatest delight at an umbrella, which my master presented him; he opened and shut it again and again, and seemed to wonder how it was made. We parted on very good terms with him, and took the road toward the kingdom of Kajaaga; but the heat of the day being quite insupportable, my master thought it better we should rest till evening and then pursue our journey, which we did. Never shall I forget, as night came on, and our road led through a thick forest : the air was quite still, and we could plainly hear the howlings of the wild beasts through the wood ; and often, as they passed near us, we could plainly see their great shadows as they stalked along. I expected every minute that they would come upon us ; and how we escaped them I know not, but that Providence was watching over us, and protected us mercifully through that dangerous night. We arrived in safety at the city of Joag. It is surrounded by a high wall, as is also each separate house. The inhabitants are an industrious people, anxious for gain, but only seeking it by honest means. We made no stop here, but travelled on till we came to the banks of the Senegal River, crossed it at a ferry, and from thence proceeded through a rich and fertile country. We soon after got into the kingdom of Kasson ; the king of which, having heard of my master's arrival, sent him a present of a milk-white bullock, which is considered a mark of great favour ; and likewise gave him full permission to pass freely through all his dominions. We stopped the next night at Soolo, but could not sleep ; for a great troop of wolves, hyenas, and other wild beasts, were prowling around the town the whole night, and the inhabitants were all endeavouring to drive them off. It is remarkable, that the approach of these animals was made known to them by the dismal howling that all the dogs of the village set up ; and this, the people told me, was always a sure sign of it to them.

"But how, Tom, did they drive them away?"

"By lighting large fires, shouting and hallooing, and running about with bunches of blazing grass in their hands. Indeed, the uproar they made was enough to frighten more than the wild beasts. The next day we travelled on, following the windings of the river Krieko, through a highly cultivated country, where provisions were so cheap, that at a market town I saw, I don't know how much corn and milk was bought for a few beads. In our way to the town of Kemmo, we were tempted to ride into a small thicket, in hopes of gathering some fruit. We were surprised at the appearance of two negroes on horseback, who, however, were excessively frightened at us. The nearer we came to them the more they were alarmed, till at last one of them rode off at full speed, and the other, as you may be sure, did not long stay behind. This amused us exceedingly; and, indeed, if you had seen the wild-looking creatures they were, you would have thought it more natural that we should fly from them.

"Unfortunately for us, our road, after this, led through a Moorish kingdom, where the inhabitants (I mean the Moors themselves) are unfeeling and insolent in the extreme. A party of them surrounded, and actually attacked the hut in which we lodged; hissed, shouted at, and abused us, and at length seized on all our baggage. It was in vain for us to make any resistance. They did not carry off our things, but had the impudence to open them before our eyes, and help themselves to whatever they took a fancy to.

"You may readily suppose we made our escape from this place at as early an hour as possible the next morning, and arrived on a great feast-day at a neighbouring town, where the people were amusing themselves with singing and dancing, and all kinds of merriment. This lively scene revived our spirits a little, for we felt quite cast down and unhappy at the ill treatment we had received, and at my poor master losing such a quantity of things that were of so much value to him. However, there was no help for that now, so we had only to make the best of it. The people stopped their dance to gaze at us for awhile; and indeed we should willingly have stayed to look on at their sports and feasting, but my master wished to go to the Moorish king's camp, to ask for compensation for all his losses, and to request his protection.

"We found a great number of dirty-looking tents pitched in a wide open plain; but instead of being protected as we hoped, what was our astonishment when the people rudely came in crowds about us, and pressed upon us, so that we were nearly suffocated! We were greatly fatigued after our journey, and suffered dreadfully from heat and thirst, but they took no pity on us: and this was all before the king himself.

who quietly sat in his tent while we were enduring this hardship; he caused us to be plundered of almost every thing we had about us, and when we begged to be allowed to go away, glad to escape with our lives, he flatly refused to let us stir one step, and informed us we were now his prisoners! Our hearts died within us at this; but we thought our best chance of safety was to submit quietly.

" And here we might have remained for ever, had it not happened that the queen expressed a great curiosity to see us; and we were led before her, just as you would lead a monkey about as a show. She seemed to take pity on us, and gave us with her own hand a drink of milk each, which was a mark of great favour. Encouraged by her kindness, my master at length ventured to request her to speak to the king in our behalf; and, in a very short time afterward, we were granted our liberty; and besides that, our horses and a great part of our baggage were given back to us. Nothing could equal our joy, and, as you may be sure, we lost no time in setting out on our journey; but here we suffered dreadfully from both hunger and thirst, for we had no provisions with us, and the fear of falling again into the hands of the Moors made us avoid every habitation, choosing rather to subsist on whatever herbs and fruits we could meet with on our way: but our road lay through a very desert country, and we began soon to suffer from want of water; this grew worse and worse every mile we went. We met some shepherd boys, with their flocks, and asked them to show us the way to the nearest spring, but they told us, to our grief, that they had not themselves seen any water in the woods. We had nothing for it but to travel on. One time I climbed to the top of a high tree, to look about me, and see if there was any hope for us at all; but nothing was to be seen all around but a dreary stretch of barren sandy soil. I put up a prayer to Almighty God to have mercy upon us, and fixed all my hopes on his goodness. My poor master fainted, and, I thought, was at the point of death, when it seemed, all at once, as if Heaven heard my prayers; for a slight thunder-storm came on, attended with heavy rain. This revived us; we spread out our clothes upon the ground, and when they were completely soaked, we quenched our thirst, by sucking the water from them. Our extreme thirst being thus somewhat allayed, we began to suffer from hunger. We again looked to that almighty Power who had so lately sent us relief, believing that he would not forsake us; and in a short time afterward perceiving, to our great joy, the smoke of a village rising at a distance, we hastened to it. A poor woman sat spinning, with a distaff, at the door of the nearest cottage, and we begged from her a morsel of bread. She instantly fetched us some, giving us, at the same time, a delicious drink of goat's milk. Nothing could be kinder than her hospitality; and though, in the rest of our journey, we often suffered from hunger and thirst, we never failed to get relief, even from the poorest negro, who sometimes had scarcely enough for himself.

"As we passed the town of Kabla, the natives were busily employed in gathering the fruit of the shea tree, for the purpose of making from it a vegetable butter, which keeps good the whole year, without salt. It is whiter, firmer, and richer flavoured than the best dairy butter I ever tasted, on which account the shea tree is highly valued by the natives. It looks, my master said, like the American oak, and bears a fruit like a Spanish olive. The kernel, from which the butter is procured, is found inside a greenish pulp, covered with a thick rind.

"After having lodged at a town to which the Moors bring salt, beads, and coral, to exchange for gold dust and cotton cloth, we again set forward, and reached Modiboo the next evening. On our way we saw a cameleopard trotting quietly before us, no way afraid of pursuit. This animal is so tall, that a man on horseback could stand between his fore legs, but he is perfectly harmless. Here also we had a fine view of the Niger, the object of my master's curiosity, stretching east and west. I was glad, for his sake, to see it; but often did I wish myself many a mile from it. The air on its banks is so filled with moschetoes that it was impossible to rest: our clothes were torn to rags, so that we had no defence from their stings, and we were obliged to walk about the whole night, fanning ourselves with our hats.

"For two days more we advanced to the eastward, it being my master's intention, if possible, to reach Tombuctoo, which we heard was not many days' journey farther on. We had no food, nor money to buy it; we were without clothes to screen us from the weather, and the rainy season had set in; but, to crown all, my poor master, whose constitution, however strengthened by habit, was not proof against all we endured, fell sick of a dangerous fever. For many days his life was in danger. However, he did recover, although slowly, and all thoughts of pursuing our journey having been abandoned, we resolved, without delay, to turn our steps to the place whence we had set out. In order to avoid Sego, we followed the Niger, getting on with great difficulty, from the floods caused by the rains, so that we often waded breast high, and more than once our horses stuck in the mud, and were near perishing The cruel Moors had prejudiced the whole country against us; so that, although we passed by a great many towns and villages, they were unwilling to give us food; and but for the humanity of a few negroes, we must have starved.

"We did not always follow the windings of the river. At one time, quitting the strand, and crossing some hills which lay in our way, we entered a peaceful village, called Kooma, belonging to a Mandingo merchant. He was a kind man. The villagers look up to him as a father and the weary are always welcome under his roof. Here we rested some time, until my master had recovered strength enough to set out upon his journey. We felt the necessity, however, of returning, and after taking grateful leave of our kind host, set out for Sibidoloo, over a steep and rocky road. On our way thither, we were attacked by a party of robbers, who left us nothing but our shirts, trowsers, and hats. In this state we entered Sibidoloo, and my master having made his case known to the dooly, or chief man, he took the pipe from his mouth, and said, " Sit down, you shall have every thing restored to you. I have said it—stay here till you receive them." My master was unwilling to remain a burden upon him; the scarcity of food being very great. To our surprise, however, the horses and clothes were returned in less than a week. We therefore immediately set out; for though we were sure of suffering from hunger, we could not expect those to give us food who had scarcely any for themselves.

" After wandering from village to village, half fed and almost naked, we came to Kamalia, where my master made acquaintance with a slatee, or slave merchant, who was collecting a coffle, or caravan of slaves, in order to sell them at Gambia. In the course of conversation, he told us of a curious little book that had been given him by an English merchant; he still had it in his possession, but had never found any body able to read it. . I shall not attempt to describe my master's delight when he found it to be an English prayer-book; the ease with which he read it gave the slatee a high opinion of his abilities, so that he begged us to stay till he should set out with his coffle, when we could travel safely under his protection. This was too kind an offer to be refused; he placed us, accordingly, in a clean hut, furnished us with mats for sleeping on, an earthen jar for water, and a drinking cup: these accommodations, simple as they may appear, were to us the greatest luxuries, after all we had suffered.

"In Kamalia, and under the protection of this man, we remained until he was ready to set out with his coffle. Why should I distress you by saying that thirty-five of our fellow-creatures were yoked in pairs, neck to neck, and in that way conducted to Pisania? However, to abridge my narrative. After a journey, without accident, and distinguished by nothing but the sufferings of our poor fellow-travellers, we reached the end of our toils, and saw ourselves once more under the hospitable roof of the English merchants who had so kindly assisted my master before we set out."

"But tell me what kind of drink do the Africans take with their meals? for I don't think I have heard that from you yet."

"The usual drink," answered Thomas, "of the inhabitants of the part of Africa where we now were is water; but they make a beverage which resembles our beer, and is extremely pleasant. The grain made use of for this purpose is a kind of millet, which is prepared like our malt, and to the juice they add a bitter, which gives it a very agreeable taste.

" They also extract a juice from several trees: but that which yields the greatest quantity, and is most liked, is a kind of palm, which rises to the height of sixty feet, or more. A good tree of this kind, I have been informed, will give ten or twelve pounds of juice, which, if drank immediately, is sweet and mild; but if kept for twenty-four hours, it ferments, becomes sharp, and would make a man who took it freely as drunk as wine."

"I have been thinking, Tom," says old Jackson, " that there is very little of the western coast of Africa known; for though you have now led me around this great quarter of the world, you have said nothing, I remark, concerning the western shore: from the Cape of Good Hope to the Gambia is more than three thousand miles, and yet you have not mentioned a single place in all that great distance. I think, if there had been any part of it worth visiting, your master would have contrived to get to it."

" Yes, father, there are, as I heard at Pisania, settlements on the coast; one at Sierra Leone, and another at Bulama, on the River Grande: These are both south of the Gambia. There is also one belonging to the French at Senegal, south of the same river. All these, however, though many years established, have made but little progress inland, and may be almost said to be still in their infancy. That at Sierra Leone was established for the benevolent purpose of restoring to their native country a number of negroes, who, having been carried away from Africa, when very young, as slaves, and afterward becoming free, wished to return. It was intended they should act as merchants between their countrymen and Europe, and persuade them not to kidnap their neighbours for the purpose of selling them as slaves, but rather to be industrious in raising those articles of produce which they could exchange for our goods.*

" Notwithstanding a great many disappointments, the settlement of Sierra Leone still exists ; and it is getting gradually over those prejudices which at first opposed it. You must see, however, that it offered no great inducement to a traveller to go there. But while we stayed at Pisania we heard of a kingdom called Ashantee ; and if the account of it which we heard was true, it well deserves to be mentioned. The capital of Ashantee is Coomassie, one hundred and fifty miles from a small English settlement called Cape Coast Castle ; and an em-

* We perceive that our friend Thomas has omitted to mention the American colony at Liberia. This is a district on the western coast of Africa, extending two hundred and eighty miles in length, and from twenty to thirty miles in breadth, and is in the vicinity of the English settlement at Sierra Leone. The climate is represented as serene ; the soil deep, rich, and fertile. It is watered by numerous rivers. A portion of this country was purchased in 1821 by the American Colonization Society, for the purpose of colonizing such manumitted slaves, or free persons of colour, as were desirous of returning to the land of their forefathers. The colony is prosperous.—Am. Ed.

bassy was sent thither to make a treaty of peace with the king; his subjects being in the habit of making attacks on the people who lived under the English protection. When the embassy arrived, it was met by no less than five thousand warriors, with music, horns, drums, rattles, gongs, added to the firing of muskets, and the shouts of the crowds. The dress of the warriors was a helmet, with gilded rams' horns, decked out with plumes of eagles' feathers, and fastened under their chins with bands of shells; the vest was red cloth, adorned with gold and silver; leopards' tails hung down their backs, and from different parts of their bodies were hung small brass bells, which jingled as they moved. They wore loose cotton trowsers, with red leather boots; a small quiver of poisoned arrows hung from their waist, and they carried a small spear in their left hand, covered with red cloth and silk tassels. As the party advanced toward the king's palace, the streets were crowded with spectators; and the open porches before the houses were filled with females and children, anxious to see the white men. Indeed, the whole account is so like what is represented on the stage, that my master was inclined to doubt the truth of it, but he was assured it was the fact. These people are remarkable for their cleanly habits; and their houses are as clean as their persons. The Ashantee loom is like ours, and they make in it cloth of great fineness. They paint, are good goldsmiths, and excel in pottery; they are also very good carpenters. But this is the best side of the picture. They are fierce, and, in some of their customs, more barbarous than you would expect to find people with such a knowledge of the arts. On their great festivals they often put a number of persons to death, having first tortured them with the most ingenious cruelty. Some of their festivals take place every twenty days, and there are not fewer than one hundred sacrificed at each. On the death of the king's mother, no less than one hundred were butchered. The party were required to be present at one of these bloody executions; but they were obliged to force their way out, being no longer able to witness such a review. How wicked, thought I, is the human heart when under the dominion of superstition and ignorance! and how happy it would be for this people if some of those good men who have carried the gospel of peace to the Hottentots could lead the poor Ashantees to the possession of that true religion which teaches love to God and love to our neighbour, and shows us that if we hope for mercy we must be merciful ourselves!

"Thus ended my adventures in Africa. When we reached Pisania, from which we had been eighteen months absent, we were received with great kindness. Our absence had been so much more protracted than my master had expected, that they supposed we must have been cut off by some of the Moorish nations in our course; and they were the more certain of this from the number of travellers who had perished when attempting the same route. Our wearing apparel had been kept safely for us, so that we both put on the English dress, never again, I hope, to exchange it for that of any other nation, and had our venerable beards shaved. For my own part, I did not regret the loss of this troublesome appendage, but it was curious to hear some of the natives, who had seen us before we cut them off; they said we were suddenly changed from men to boys; and, I confess, though I disliked a long beard reaching down to my breast, I thought it did produce that change in us. A few days after, an American vessel setting sail, we took our passage in her for Charleston, North America, and meeting at sea with a West-Indiaman, bound for England, we shifted into her, and, after a pleasant though slow passage, arrived in Falmouth.

"Here I took leave of my kind master, who, on all occasions, had treated me more like a friend than his servant; indeed, I can truly say I looked upon him as both; for, in all our sufferings, he was ever ready to give me the kindest advice, as well as to talk with me about every thing that struck him as worth attention. When we were parting he paid me my wages in full, though on several occasions he had advanced me small sums on account; in addition to which he gave me a most liberal present. 'Go home now, Jackson,' said he, 'and share with your parents what you have made. You have told me your story, and you know I never con cealed from you my opinion that you were wrong in becoming discontented with your situation, and wrong also in leaving the shelter of your father's roof, on the wild scheme of seeking your fortune.' And surely, father, he was right. It is true, the Almighty has, in his mercy, brought me safe through a great many dangers, and sent me home with the means of making your last days happy; but this should be no encouragement to those who have a roving disposition to follow my example. Jem Hobson left home along with me, and it pleased God that he should never return to it. I have, therefore, learned one great truth, which I would gladly recommend to every one who reads my travels; it is short, and might well be written in letters of gold:—'*With industry and contentment we may be happy in the humblest station; and, whatever befalls us, let us trust in the Almighty, whose arm is powerful to save. He doth all things well; he knoweth what is good for us, and he hath promised to guide those who look to him for wisdom.*'

"With such opinions as these, Tom," said the old man, the tears rising to his eyes as he spoke, "I no longer regret your cruel departure and your long absence. Had you returned to me poor as you left me, but blest with such wisdom as this, I should say you were returned as rich as I could desire. Wealth, Tom, may belong to the worthless—and many a time we see it denied to the deserving; but there is one thing which money cannot buy, nor poverty take away; it is that which gives us peaceful sleep, and happy thoughts while we are awake; it is that, Tom, which you must have often felt the want of; for often and often you accused yourself, I warrant, of your undutiful desertion of your parents; need I say that the possession of which I speak, and which we should desire most to obtain, is that of *a good conscience.*"

THE END.

www.ingramcontent.com/pod-product-compliance
Lightning Source LLC
Chambersburg PA
CBHW020308170426
43202CB00008B/538